GARDENS FOR THE SENSES

GARDENING AS THERAPY

BY

HANK BRUCE

Hank Bruce
30548 St Andrews Blvd.
Sorrento, FL 32776
(352) 383-2704
hankbruce@mail2.lcia.com

D0813881

ISBN 0-932855-57-1

Published by Winner Enterprises
On the web: www.winnerenterprises.com
Or send e-mail to: info@winnerenterprises.com

Illustrations by Hank Bruce
Editorial: Erv Lampert
Composition: Daniel Lampert Communications

PHOTO CREDITS
Front Cover:
Rose Bush in Bloom © 1993 Tomi Jill Folk
Author's Mother, Wilhelmina Bruce © 1997 Tomi Jill Folk
Flower Garden © 1993 Tomi Jill Folk
Author's Daughter, Karen © 1974 Marlene Bruce
Back Cover: Josie in the Herb Garden © 1998 Tomi Jill Folk
Text:
Page 8, Gardener Gone to Pot, created by Traci Anderson
© 1999 Hank Bruce
Page 32, Container Garden © 1991 Hank Bruce
Page 110, Author and grandson, Alex Bainbridge, enjoying
Marigolds © 1998 Tomi Jill Folk

Printed in the United States of America

Thanks

A book isn't created as much as it is grown. This one was nurtured by the encouraging words of Gene Rothert of the Chicago Botanical Gardens and past president of the American Horticultural Therapy Association, John Matthes, past president of the Florida Chapter of the AHTA, Sheila Kelly, president of the Florida Chapter of the AHTA. The seed was planted by Katy Moss Warner, General Manager of Horticulture at Walt Disney World, who suggested that there might be value is such a book. Ben Brogdon, Sam Lemheney, Wendy Andrew and Kristin Pategas of Walt Disney World's unequaled horticulture staff also nurtured this project.

The book was patiently pruned to shape by my wife, Tomi Jill Folk, and its publisher, Erv Lampert of Winner Enterprises. The input of many horticultural therapists, clients and members of the community provided the bright safe environment where it could grow to fruition.

Thank you all, very much. This couldn't have happened without you.

This book isn't designed to give the reader all the answers. The fact is that for many aspects of the connections between plants and humanity, we don't even know the questions yet. The knowledge that gardens, gardening and nature are therapeutic to the body, mind and soul is nothing new. But the dimensions of application are expanding as we learn more, enter into the quest to understand more about ourselves and our place in the global web of life we call home. The author's primary objective is simply to generate some thoughtful reflection and encourage some escape to the reality of the garden. Perhaps hand in hand we can find peace and harmony as we experience our gardens.

Thank you for reading *Gardens for the Senses: Gardening as Therapy.*

TABLE OF CONTENTS

All Gardens Are Sensory   *Page 5*
All Gardening Is Therapeutic   6
Gardening in the New Millennium   7

Part 1.   GARDENS FOR THE SENSES   10
          Appealing to the Senses   10
          The Scratch & Sniff Landscape   12
          A Matter of Taste   21
          A Sight to Behold   31
          Hearing the Garden's Song   37
          In Touch with the Garden   39
          Beyond Our Physical Senses   45
Part 2.   GARDENING AS THERAPY   51
          The Therapeutic Garden   53
          Therapy for the Body   55
          Therapy for the Mind   63
          Therapy for the Soul   74
Part 3.   PUTTING IT ALL TOGETHER   80
          Special Populations   80
          Children, Developmentally Disabled,
          Limited Mobility
          The Socially Disadvantaged and HT   96
          Community Gardens, Without a Home,
          Prison Gardens, Drugs & Alcohol,
          Abuse Victims and Abusers
          Senior Populations   102
          Alzheimer's Patients, End of Life and HT
          Special Gardens   109
          Scratch & Sniff Gardens, The Touch Pool,
          The Night Garden
          Horticultural Therapy in Tomorrow's World   115
          Resources and Information   117

All Gardens Are Sensory

That is, every garden appeals to, and affects, our senses. We all see, feel, smell or taste the wonders of life that make the landscape, the backyard, the vegetable garden, the park almost magnetic to our souls.

We are instinctively drawn to the mystery, security, beauty, comfort, and promise of tomorrow that these special places provide. Few are the people who can walk through a park or botanical garden and not stop to smell the flowers, touch bark and leaves, listen to the breezes as they give the leaves voice and motion, or watch the butterflies. The garden is an ever changing kaleidoscope of life in a safe corner of our world.

We describe this sensory experience as either active or passive. Many of us need to be engaged in the "partnership of growth" that requires us to feel and smell the moist earth as well as appreciate the drama and beauty of the landscape. But even for those who enjoy horticulture by strolling through a botanical garden or arboretum, it is not a totally passive exercise. We can't help ourselves. We inhale the multitude of scents. We hear the breeze, birds, water, and, yes, even the bugs.

Instinctively we reach out, even when the signs sternly tell us not to, and touch the leaves or bark, caress the petal. By employing all these senses we stimulate the body, mind and spirit. We see in our mind images from the past, feel comforted, uplifted and inspired. In the garden we see the reality of life from birth to death and regeneration. The mind is actively engaged, even if the hands are not. The mind is never passive in the garden.

All Gardening Is Therapeutic

To stroll through a garden is to soothe the troubled soul, lose the accumulated stress of daily life, to exercise the body, stimulate the mind. There are professional horticultural therapists who work with residents of nursing homes, hospital patients, hospice caregivers, people with physical and mental disabilities, school programs, prisons, abuse victims and abusers, drug and alcohol treatment programs, and many other special populations.

This is nothing new. This is ancient wisdom that's being rediscovered by the health care professions. In Egypt of the pharaohs, depressed and mentally ill members of the court were taken on leisurely strolls through the royal gardens. In medieval Spain, poor hospital patients worked in the gardens to pay their bills. These patients had better recovery rates than the wealthy who didn't spend time in the gardens. Physically and mentally wounded soldiers in WWI were helped with "garden therapy." The tension and discord of entire communities has been healed when the residents cooperated to create gardens and parks.

This therapeutic role of gardening isn't limited to professionals working with handicapped populations. Every one of us can reap the therapeutic benefits of gardening for ourselves. Whether we are tilling a 1/2 acre garden, caring for a couple of fruit trees, tending a few plants on the patio or windowsill, or watching a butterfly garden, we can both know the joy and share the excitement.

The purists draw a distinction between horticulture as therapy and gardening as a pleasant pastime. They insist that we must be disabled before gardening can be considered therapeutic. But who among us is so healthy and mentally stable that we don't need some healing? Not only can we all benefit from this kind of therapy, we can also be our own therapist.

We can wait for someone to bring us flowers,
or we can plant our own, and grow with them.

Gardening in the New Millennium

As we enter a new century and a new millennium, we are also entering a new era of gardening. In the 20th century, we assumed an adversarial role with the natural world. We chose to battle the elements, wage war on weeds, practice genocide on insects and other animals. Everything natural was the enemy. We turned farm and field into wasteland and poisoned our backyards with pesticides in our lust to control. We failed to understand that while it appears that nature is aggressive and predatory, it's more often cooperative and interdependent. No part of nature stands alone, and this is a good lesson for all of us.

We made the yard a war zone, the garden a battlefield. We killed off the songbirds when we poisoned the bugs. We almost destroyed our national symbol, the bald eagle, by failing to understand the cumulative effect DDT was having on its food chain. Because of pollutants we don't yet understand, populations of amphibians and birds all over the world are declining. When we killed the bugs, we also killed the butterflies.

The good news is that we are regaining our sense of balance. We are beginning to comprehend the simple fact that humanity is a part of nature, not apart from it. Nature isn't the enemy. We are learning that there are both great joys and immense rewards to be had when we accept our place in the sun and share the wonder of it all.

As competition gives way to cooperation, and we discover that acquisition is such a heavy burden that sharing is a better way to live, we will find greater peace of mind. The active participation with the reality of our being is far better than the virtual existence we attempted to create with our gardens of the 20th century.

Gardening is something to be enjoyed, a labor of love, not a series of obstacles to be overcome or enemies to be defeated. Gardening is an art, a means of creative expression, a shared experience with God, and a never ending journey of discovery.

It isn't problems; it's possibilities. Gardening will be joy not chore, exercise not work, pleasure not punishment. This is a change that is taking place now, as we begin to understand those simple words *peace* and *harmony.* In yesterday's gardens our instinctive people-plant connections were nurtured. Past generations knew the comfort of being a part of something bigger than themselves without feeling the drive to dominate, overpower, defeat nature.

When we accept our place in the garden, it becomes a place of healing, a place of discovery, a source of therapy for the body, mind and soul. You and I can make the garden a gym, a library, a sanctuary. We can make tomorrow an exciting place to be.

Whimsey for the Soul

Gardening is a Gateway to Reality

The traditional English garden of a century ago was designed to dispel melancholy. In that gray climate, the beauty of color and fragrance was essential, and it continues to be so today. The therapeutic value of plants isn't limited to the great outdoors. The windowsill, patio, plant stand or entryway can be a comfortable place that can be enjoyed every day of the year.

Plants are non-judgmental. They don't care what your economic status is, the color of your skin, or how much education you've had. They don't care if a seeing eye dog is your constant companion, or if you get around in a wheelchair. They'll gladly share their space with you and reward you for the care you give them.

If the promise of leaf, flower and fruit lies within the dustlike seed, then what promise within the human heart?

PART ONE
GARDENS FOR THE SENSES

But nothing could exceed the freshness and beauty of the
flowers, still loaded as they were with the moisture of the
night, and this mysterious and shadowy hour of dawn, when
they open, as if to ...shed those sweetest perfumes ...
George Sand

Chapter 1
Appealing to the Senses

Gardening is a sensual experience. That is, one can't stroll through a garden without becoming a part of it, because all of the senses are affected. We cannot refuse to accept the fragrance of the rose, the lilac or the jasmine. The flower becomes the atmosphere. We breath it, we seek it out when we stoop to swim in the aroma of peonies, or reach to grasp with both the hand and the soul the gentle power of wildflowers in bloom.

Who doesn't react to the smell of vine ripened tomatoes, warmed in the afternoon sun. The fruity aroma of peaches, strawberries, oranges, apples, grapes and so many more speak to us of sustenance and survival. The delightful aromas of fresh fruits and vegetables are promises of another body-satisfying sensory experience to follow. So much of our garden experience goes beyond our sense of smell to include the sense of taste.

We cannot resist the urge to touch the velvet leaves of mullein, or the waxy petals of a cactus blossom. To feel the bark of trees, the texture of a lotus leaf, the burr of a chestnut or the cap of an acorn is a private journey of discovery.

The garden isn't a silent place. There's the voice of the wind and the whisper of breezes as they journey through the leaves. The songs of other visitors, birds, frogs, squirrels, and insects are a reminder that we do not own, but only share the garden. We can be both soothed and invigorated by the sound of water in motion. The garden is filled with sound, if we are only willing to be quiet enough to hear, and still enough to become a part of it.

Beauty isn't limited to what can be seem by the eye, but the sense of sight is one of the key ways we experience the garden. We marvel at the diversity of color and form. The visual beauty is found in the single frond of a fern and the drama of a forest or meadow.

We don't have to know the botanical nomenclature, or the evolutionary saga of the plants in our garden. All we need to do is learn how to experience and enjoy them, to share the mystery and wonder of life itself with them.

The human mind hates to be bored. In an experiment conducted several years ago, people were placed in dark, soundproof isolation tanks where they could only lie motionless in a few inches of warm salt water. Within hours these human Guinea pigs began to hallucinate. The human mind cannot tolerate being bored. Sometimes we can stimulate one or two of the senses without experiencing the others. Listening to music on the radio, or watching a movie on TV, employs our sense of hearing, and in the case of the TV program, sight; but we can't touch the instruments, inhale the new car smell of the commercial, or share in the taste of the fine wine the actors seem to be enjoying. We can use our imagination to be a part of the experience, though. We don't have to experience every object or event with all of our senses, but gardening does give us a great opportunity to use more of them than TV. In the garden, we experience reality. That's part of the joy of it.

How fair is a garden amid the toils and passions of existence.
Benjamin Disraeli

Chapter 2
The Scratch & Sniff Landscape

Our sense of smell is a time machine. The scent of a lilac may trigger memories of a childhood long forgotten, transporting us back through the years to some special warm spring morning. Each of us has a multitude of olfactory memory bytes stored in our mind. Scientists tell us this is a survival skill that has served us well. There is logic in this. We are warned by the negative odors of spoiled food or polluted water, attracted by the fragrance of ripening fruit. The aromas of certain flowers and foliage tell us when it's time to plant, or harvest, or time that young children can go barefoot.

One elderly lady, an Alzheimer's patient, would relate delightful stories of her childhood Christmases every time she smelled oranges. It seemed that she had grown up in a very poor family. Christmas was the only time of the year they got oranges; in fact, some years that was the only Christmas gift for the children. An aunt of mine could describe in perfect detail the farmhouse of her early childhood when these memories were triggered by fresh spearmint. She had the childhood job of cutting mint and spreading it throughout the house as an air freshener.

Our sense of smell is said to be one of the most primitive senses. In most animals it's a far more developed sense than sight or hearing. There are also claims that it is one of the first senses to decline as we age, but this may be due to the fact that we have no corrective lenses for our nose. We don't have to let our ability to appreciate fragrance atrophy. There is one thing we can all do and that's so simple that it's often overlooked. We can exercise our nose. This may sound silly, but there does seem to be evidence that people who have herb gardens, rose gardens and fragrance gardens do seem to maintain their sense of smell forever. During lectures and horticultural presentations, we noticed that many of the senior citizens who didn't garden couldn't detect the aromas of pineapple sage, lemon grass, miniature roses, hyacinths and so many other delightful plants. The gardeners could describe the difference between lemon verbena and lemon eucalyptus, dianthus and carnations, even the subtle variations among roses. It seems that those of us who play in the garden not only condition our muscles, we exercise our noses as well. It's an unfortunate fact, however, that our sense of smell is destroyed by smoking, many diseases and some medications.

This ability to smell is the way we read our "chemo-sensory environment." We literally inhale minute airborne particles of the dinner being prepared, the campfire, popcorn, gasoline, tomatoes, raw sewage, garlic, mildew, fine perfume and the list could continue almost forever. These smells are literally signals to our brain, and our brain tells us how to react to them. The spicy aroma of apple pie baking, bread fresh from the oven, or a steak on the grill will trigger our salivary glands and, because dining is instinctively a social activity, the same aroma puts us in a sociable mood. Other scents may warn us of danger. We have an natural automatic dislike for the smell of pesticides, cigarette smoke, and the defensive abilities of a skunk. In these aromas we read danger.

We are capable of reading minute quantities of the volatile oils released by the flowers and foliage of our garden plants. Not only do we mentally recognize these scents, we react to them. A walk through a garden can evoke intense feelings. We once tried an experiment at a local botanical garden. I was blindfolded, then led down the paths and walkways. It is amazing how much we can experience with our sense of smell. I was able to detect fragrances and odors I hadn't noticed before. By smelling the air I could tell whether we were near the lake, the fern garden or the hickory trees. It was also interesting to note the mental images that my mind was free to form because I couldn't see what was really before me. Not only were there memories from the past, but creative images of places I have never been, perhaps places that don't really exist. Certain locations on the walk brought forth a sense of relaxation, a calm feeling. Several sites on this blindfolded tour caused a sense of apprehension, almost fear while still others were absolutely invigorating.

Throughout the world the ability of botanical scents to change moods, improve mental attitude and play a role in healing is well accepted and employed in both medicine for the body and religious practices. Many in our technological western society view these herbal cures as primitive nonsense and superstition. Yet we cannot deny the magic to be found in a dozen long-stemmed red roses, can we? Is the perfume industry, a major segment of our global economy, based on superstition? We naturally, instinctively, respond to the scent of honeysuckle, patchouli, gardenia, ginger, or allspice, with a smile and a sense of well being. Romantic moods are triggered not only by the visual appearance of stephanotis and roses, but the fragrance.

In a study done years ago, a group of blindfolded college students were presented with a number of fragrant botanical oils on cotton balls. They recorded the mental images that each scent evoked. The results indicated that the responses were almost universal. Calming images were generated when they inhaled the scent of lavender, oranges or chamomile. Roses, vanilla and chocolate brought romantic images to mind. Allspice made them smile as they envisioned activity and joy.

In research done in a dormitory study area, the scent of peppermint, basil, rosemary and lemongrass were released to various groups of students as they prepared for tests. Control groups were exposed to none of these fragrances. During the exam, the same scents were released in the classroom. The aroma triggered memories from the earlier study time and these students scored higher than the control group that hadn't received the olfactory stimuli.

The concept of "aroma therapy" isn't some new age fad, nor is it an answer to every physical or mental distress. Because fragrances and scents do trigger emotional responses, there is logic in exploring the value of rosemary to soothe and invigorate, allspice to bring smiles, and peppermint to dispel melancholy.

Our nose doesn't have a long attention span, however. After a few minutes of exposure to a new odor, our brain has made all the value judgments it needs to about it, and begins to look for something else to play with, examine or creatively think about. This isn't to say that a strong scent doesn't stay with us, it simply means that it tends to take a back seat to new stimuli.

Simply working with aromatic plants, even strolling through a fragrance garden or tending a windowsill herb garden is therapeutic. These nasal stimulations, imagination instigations and time transportations don't have to be limited to a few weeks in the spring. There are enough aromatic plants to make the entire year a sensory delight.

We can incorporate this olfactory dimension into our gardens without much effort. Many of the plants we already grow in our landscape give a wide range of floral and foliar scents. Fortunately, there are always opportunities to expand the use of aromatic plants, both indoors and out.

Dianthus

Tips on using aromatic plants

- Plants with aromatic foliage are most effective when they aren't grown side by side. If too many scents are in close proximity, each one loses its identity.
- There is no need to isolate all the aromatic plants in a separate garden. They can be distributed throughout the landscape, and they're more effective that way.
- Aromatic plants are at their best when they're a discovery, not a destination. The role of mystery in the garden is one of its most mentally stimulating aspects.
- With a little planning, there can be garden scents throughout the year. Fragrance isn't limited to lilac and roses.
- The fragrance of the garden can be brought indoors in the form of bouquets or potpourri.
- There's a multitude of aromatic plants that enjoy life on the windowsill or lighted plant stand.

Use the lists below to help plan your "scratch & sniff" garden. Keep in mind that these are only suggestions, points of departure. After all, it is your backyard, your windowsill, your landscape. You have the final word on what grows there.

Top 10 Fragrant Flowering Plants

Chrysanthemum	Lilac
Clove pinks (carnations)	Lily-of-the-valley
Confederate jasmine	Orange Blossom
Gardenia	Rose
Honeysuckle	Stocks (evening scented)

Top 10 Plants with Aromatic Foliage

Anise hyssop	Lavender
Basil	Marigold
Chives	Mints (many varieties)
Dill	Rosemary
Fennel	Thyme

Fragrance on the Windowsill

Carnation
Chives
Dwarf citrus
Gardenia
Geranium, scented leaf

Miniature rose
Parsley
Plectranthus
Rosemary
Thyme

Fragrance of the Tropics

Allspice
Camphor tree
Gardenia
Ginger
Jasmine

Lemon tree (all citrus)
Natal plum, dwarf
Nightblooming jasmine
Plumeria
Stephanotis

Aromas for All Seasons

Bayberry
Cedar
Juniper
Pines
Wax Myrtle
Wintergreen
Witch hazel

Desert Fragrance

Chamisa
Chaparral
Creosote bush
Catclaw acacia
Desert willow
Desert four o'clock
Sacred Datura

Trees with Fragrance

Apple blossom
Black locust
Citrus
Eucalyptus
Fringe tree

Linden
Russian olive
Sourwood
Sweet acacia
Sweet viburnum (V. Carlsi)

Rosemary

Aromatic Plants that Discourage Insects

Chives

Citrosa

Eucalyptus (many varieties)

Garlic

Geraniums

Iboza (African Moth plant)

Marigolds (French dwarf)

Pennyroyal

Rosemary

Tansy

Aromatic Bedding Plants

Alyssum, sweet

Angel's trumpet (datura)

Dianthus

Marigold

Mignonette

Nicotiana (flw tobacco)

Petunia

Stocks

Sweet pea

Perennials

Agastache

Daphne odora

Four O'clocks

Hyssop

Lavender

Lilies (many)

Lantana

Peonies

Tuberose

I know a bank where the wild thyme blows,
Where oxlips and the nodding violet grows,
Quite over-canopied with luscious woodbine,
With sweet musk-roses and with eglantine: . . .
Bill Shakespeare, "Midsummer Night's Dream"

Old-fashioned rose

Aromatic foliage and fragrant flowers do stimulate our senses, make us feel good, even force involuntary smiles to cross our faces. Few among us can resist the temptation to stoop and smell a flower we don't know. We seek an olfactory clue to its identity as a way of indexing it in our memory files, but we are also displaying the courage to explore the unknown, make a discovery, experience something new, live the mystery of life. We sniff the fragrance of old and familiar floral friends to anticipate the past as we call forth pleasant memories, but also to experience the present with as many of our senses as possible, to know the pleasure and joy of the moment.

For these reasons alone they earn a place in our indoor and outdoor landscapes. But aromatic plants, the heady fragrance of flowers, the release of volatile oils from the leaves have a second value in the garden. Tomato leaves smell the way they do to discourage browsing animals. Rabbits may relish the carrots, lettuce and beets in your garden, but they will usually leave the tomatoes for the hornworms. Bean beetles and potato bugs, as is the case with most insects, are drawn to their dinner table by the aroma. If we pause to think about this for a moment, we can probably list people we know who respond in the same way.

Bugs have a pathetic little excuse for a brain. Logic tells us we should be able to outsmart them. At least that was the opinion of a high school student neighbor of mine. She was a brilliant and budding scholar who was shocked and appalled at the chemical arsenal with which her parents waged war against their six-legged foes. Being not only intelligent but efficient as well, she conducted the following experiments for a biology class report while attempting to free her backyard from chemical dependency.

First she determined what horrible monsters it was that struck terror into the hearts of Mom & Dad. She soon had a "Ten Least Wanted" list that included bean beetles, tomato hornworms, squash beetles, white flies, mites and a variety of aphids. Early one morning, while her parents slept, this intrepid teen crept into the garden and planted marigold seeds in several rows of beans, and basil seeds around some

19

of the tomatoes, leaving others as a control. She placed pots of mint, rosemary and chives among some of the cucumber and squash vines. She even went so far as to plant chives around a few of her mother's precious roses, the same roses that the Japanese beetles enjoyed so much. First her father raised serious objections to the herbs in his vegetable garden, but he relented in the name of science. He was certain that a couple weeks would be sufficient to prove his daughter wrong. Mom wasn't quite as understanding about the chives in the roses, but in the end she also negotiated a truce with the scientist-in-training.

Within weeks the marigolds were showing yellow and orange dots all over the rows of beans. Every Saturday morning found this junior scientist and her two parental lab assistants doing bug counts in the garden. The third week into the experiment they found seven bean beetle larvae in the marigold/beans along with three ladybugs. In the control rows, where there were no marigolds they counted 138 bean beetle kids and sixteen ladybugs.

The squash surrounded by rosemary and mint had no squash beetles, while over a dozen were captured on the control plants. The real surprise came with the rose bushes, however. In the area where there were no chives, the Japanese beetles had nibbled on almost every bud and leaf, while on the plants surrounded by chives there was minimal damage. There were also no aphids, but there were beautiful flowers.

Placing these aromatic plants amongst the vegetables confused the bugs. They smelled marigolds, not beans. They flocked to the squash that didn't smell like mint, and the tomatoes that hadn't been seasoned with basil. It would only be fair to mention that several of the marigolds fell victim to spider mites, but the basil that was growing closest to the tomato plants wasn't troubled by slugs, while the more isolated plants did become dinner. If we are willing to blend our herb and vegetable gardens into the landscape, we can use the plants themselves to control pests and predators rather than resorting to chemicals and poisons that have absolutely no therapeutic value to the garden or the gardener.

Chapter 3
A Matter of Taste

A small child experiences and explores the world with a well developed sense of taste. Everything goes in the mouth. We can only taste sweet, salty, sour, bitter and a class of savory sensations that are known to the scientists as "umami" with our 9,000 + taste buds. Our ability to taste is affected by aging, smoking, disease and medications. Age, sex and heredity all play a role in our sense of taste, but the quality we call taste is inextricably linked to our sense of smell. It's the nose that fine tunes the mental impression of what we taste.

During a presentation to a gardening club, one of those attending took great exception to my suggestion that a garden should also appeal to our sense of taste. She was correct in stating that parents all over the world spend a great deal of time telling their children not to eat plants they don't know. This is a valid warning. There are many ornamental plants grown because of their beauty, fragrance or function that are dangerous in one way or another. In her mind the backyard was a place of danger. The vegetables for the dinner table didn't come from the garden, they came from the grocery store. The lawn was sprayed with poisons to kill the bugs and weeds, therefore the children couldn't even play in the yard. Her children have been denied not only some of the great joys of childhood, but the instinctive link to soil that comes from actually growing something that ends up on the dinner table, or having a hand in the creation of living beauty.

To taste the fruits of our labor is one of the wholesome joys of gardening, but the accidental discovery of a new flavor, or the rediscovery of one long forgotten is a special joy. While conducting a field trip in western Pennsylvania with a group of young people, we savored the delights of teaberry and sassafras twigs. The most delighted of the party was the elderly gentleman who was serving as a chaperone. After sampling a few vine ripened dewberries, he taught everyone how to sip the sweet nectar from clover blossoms.

It's dangerous to have children, Alzheimer's patients, those with mental limitations and the rest of us nibbling to our hearts content with no knowledge of what we're putting in our mouths. However, fear is no substitute for solid information. We can teach our children at an early age to only eat what their parents have positively identified. If we are using our landscape for the enjoyment of those with an inability to make sound judgments, we can control what is growing there. Alzheimer's victims often experience their environment by tasting it. There are so many safe plants that ignorance is the only reason one can give for incorporating poisonous plants into the garden.

A Garden for Tasting

The following are only some of the plants that can be used with confidence in a garden for special populations where the plant parts may be nibbled. Even here some caution should be used.

- **Fruit trees** such as apples, pears, peaches, cherries, oranges, and many others do bear a fruit that is safe and healthy. However, care must be taken to avoid consuming unripe fruit, or foliage that can cause gastric or intestinal distress, vomiting or nausea.
- **Grapes** are a healthy part of the diet, even munching on a leaf or two will cause no problem; but unripe fruit or too many leaves can cause gastric distress, vomiting and nausea.
- **Berries,** blackberries, raspberries, strawberries and blueberries are all safe, attractive, delicious and nutritious. The only danger is from the thorns that many of these berry plants employ as a defense against predators.
- **Leafy vegetables** like lettuce, beets, cabbages, kale, spinach and celery are completely safe. By growing the more colorful varieties of lettuce, chard, cabbage or kale interest can be stimulated.
- **Beans** are always popular and safe. The common green beans, yellow wax and purple pod beans can be grown in mixed beds to generate some excitement. There is no rule that each must be grown separately. While the foliage and flowers of the winged bean are tasty and edible, the

22

foliage of most beans isn't. In fact, some of the ornamental members of the bean family can be toxic.

- **Tomatoes** are delicious when they're ripe. Green tomatoes (uncooked) and the foliage do contain solanin which is toxic. While few are tempted to dine on tomato leaves, this is a fact we need to be aware of in gardens used by special populations.
- **Peppers** are colorful and available in a wide range of shapes and flavors. The sweet bell peppers and mildly hot varieties are safe for accidental consumption, but the really hot chile peppers are best avoided in gardens where special populations may be tempted by the colorful fruit.
- **Squash & cucumbers** are great plants for a "taste" garden because the fruit can be eaten safely at any size. Squash blossoms can even be munched.
- **The Herb Garden** gives us so many delightful and safe flavors. The mints, parsley, sage, rosemary and thyme occupy a prominent place in most herb gardens, but anise hyssop, lemon balm, catnip, basil, oregano, and so many others are also a delight to the taste buds. Even some of the common herbs contain natural chemicals that can be toxic when ingested. See list of dangerous plants on page 112.

Marigold

23

Dining on the Floral Delights

I had the pleasure of attending a "floral dinner" one evening with a number of other guests. It's interesting that we have such a reluctance to eating flowers when one of the most healthy foods we have available is broccoli. This and its sister vegetable, cauliflower, are both flowers. Let me take a few minutes and describe this meal for you. It began with a small salad served on massive squash blossoms. In this salad were mint blossoms, marigold petals, sage flowers, dianthus, mustard flowers and nasturtiums.

Next came the artichokes, which are the flower buds of a thistle. But the intriguing part of this was the sunflower buds that surrounded the massive succulent thistle. This was the first time I had sampled sunflower buds and they were a delight, sautéed in butter with mushroom slices and chive flowers.

Batter fried squash blossoms followed with sprigs of orange, Mexican tarragon and pink anise hyssop blossoms on the side. We were served an iced tea brewed with rose petals. A miniature red rose floated in each glass. The main course was cubed venison seasoned with calendula flowers. Baked yucca buds and broccoli were garnished with dill and radish flowers.

Dessert was a sauce of Florida cranberries (the flower buds of a member of the hibiscus family called roselle) over ginger blossom ice cream. This was topped with okra buds and candied violas.

It was an exceptional meal flavorwise. The host and hostess successfully stimulated the minds of their guests as well as the palate. I suspect that each of us who shared that delightful feast has approached dining with a more open mind since that evening. As we savored these new and unique flavors, we opened our minds and broadened our knowledge. It's interesting to note that each of the items on the menu was a traditional food in some culture somewhere in the world.

The following is a list of edible flowers you might want to try if you haven't already.

- **Anise hyssop** flowers are fuzzy little spikes of pink, lavender or white with a delightfully licorice flavor that can add so much to salads, drinks, chicken dishes, custards, puddings and ice cream. A sweet sauce of anise hyssop flowers and leaves is delightful on pancakes, too.

- **Artichokes** are labor intensive dining, but the delicate flavor and social value make them worthwhile.

- **Banana** flowers are considered a delicacy in tropical regions.

- **Bachelor's Buttons** (Centaurea cyanus) have an interesting flavor and make a colorful garnish.

- **Begonia, tuberous only.** All begonias contain oxalic acid, but tuberous varieties contain only a minute amount, as does spinach. It is still advisable to eat them in moderation. The petals are used as a flavorful garnish for vegetable dips, sorbets, and yogurts.

- **Borage** flowers are a rich blue color that can add so much to a salad or drink when used as a garnish. The subtle, almost cucumber-like, flavor of borage compliments both fruits and vegetables.

- **Calendulas** are what the Europeans recipes refer to as pot-marigolds. The delightfully tart, almost peppery flavor adds to soups, stews, meat dishes and wild game. The flowers and petals can be used as a garnish, flavorful addition to a salad or as a seasoning in vegetable dips and dressings.

- **Carnations** have a spicy clove-like fragrance and a flavor to match. They make a delightful garnish on ham, add to the flavor of teas, puddings and ice creams, sorbets and preserves. The white end of the petal is sometimes bitter and can be removed if it is overpowering, but this is not usually a problem.

- **Chamomile** flowers have been dried for use in relaxing teas for centuries.

- **Chrysanthemum** flowers are used frequently in Oriental cooking. Petals can be scattered lightly over a salad, or whole flowers can be floated in drinks, including teas.

25

- **Clover** flowers have long been enjoyed as a childhood delight. The nectar could be sipped from the individual florets. We thank the bees for clover honey, but dried red clover blossoms also make an interesting tea. Clover florets can be a colorful garnish on pancakes, waffles, puddings and ice creams.

- **Dandelion** flowers make a delicious wine, but they're also useful in cooking. While the freshly opened flowers are sweet, the green sepals and stem can be quite bitter. The dandelion is a fun flower that embodies the joy of youth. There are few among us who doesn't smile at some childhood memory involving dandelion stem chains, parachute seeds, and pollen gold chins & cheeks. The flowers add to a fresh salad, make a colorful garnish and tickle the nose in a glass of iced tea.

- **Dianthus** (pinks) makes a great tea. The flowers can be candied. You can also make "clove pinks sugar" by alternating layers of dianthus petals and sugar crystals and leaving the petals to dry for several weeks.

- **Dill** flowers form a lacy yellow umbrella that has as much flavor as the leaves and seeds. It makes a delightful garnish on salads and dips, can be used in soups, stews, and meat dishes. Dill blossoms also make a wonderful seasoning for baked potatoes.

- **English daisies** are to the British Isles what dandelions are to America, a colorful, useful, delightful plant that has the misfortune of being too easy to grow, so in its homeland it's called a weed. The flowers of the English daisy are somewhat bitter, but can impart a subtle taste to everything from salad dressings and dips to cakes, cookies and ice cream. It also makes a colorful garnish. Tips: remove the stem and all green parts of the flower, select only the newly opened blossoms and harvest early in the morning.

- **Fennel** is a beautiful plant; when it's growing well, the flower umbels look like golden fireworks and have a flavor akin to anise. These florets make an interesting addition to teas, hot or iced, add a pleasant surprise to a mundane potato or pasta salad, but come into their true glory with cookies, cakes, ice creams and apple pies.

- **Fuschia** flowers don't have much flavor, but they certainly possess the ability to brighten any dish. They are also effective as a candied flower.

- **Gardenia** blossoms are almost too aromatic to be edible, yet they can serve as a great accent or garnish. Gardenia teas, both iced and hot are delightful.

- **Geraniums** are available in a variety of flavors. The common garden variety flowers have a distinctively pungent fragrance and a flavor to match, but this can be an effective seasoning to a wide variety of dishes. Many of the scented-leaf varieties have delicate flowers that are useful in teas, baking, sorbets, yogurts, dips, vinegars and more. A few geranium flowers can add flavor to a stir fry. Note that some of the 'citronella' scented geraniums can be quite bitter. Entire cookbooks have been written on the use of the rose-scented geranium flowers.

- **Ginger** roots give us the flavor we know as ginger, but much Oriental and tropical cooking involves the use of the flowers as well. The more subtle taste of the flowers is ideal for drinks, teas, rice dishes, frozen desserts and sweet cakes. Note that not all ginger flowers are edible, make certain you are using true ginger flowers.

- **Hibiscus** flowers have a mild citrus flavor. They can be used fresh or dried to make a delightful tea. The flowers are also used raw stuffed with seafood salads etc. Shredded hibiscus flowers can be added to everything from soups to salads, fish to chicken.

- **Hollyhock** tea possesses a subtle almost lemon flavor that is best sweetened with a hint of honey. A medieval recipe calls for hollyhock blossoms in candied tarts and sweet breads.

- **Honeysuckle** produces a hauntingly fragrant blossom on a vine that doesn't know when to quit. Note: we are talking about the Japanese honeysuckle (Lonicera japonica) which is the only one that's edible. Each white flower contains a drop of super sweet nectar. If you carefully pull the blossom from the stem you can sip this juice from the tube of the flower. You can also steep the blossoms in tea, bake them into all manner of wonderful desserts, make honeysuckle sugar, garnish fruit compotes, and flavor frozen dishes with them.

- **Impatiens** are colorful and edible, but they don't have much flavor. Still they serve as a bright garnish, or as floating confetti in a punch bowl.

- **Johnny-Jump-Ups** are another of those smile inducing flowers. The flavor is subtle and sweet, just like its cousin, the violet. Some claim to taste wintergreen, but it seems to me that it has a minty flavor all its own. These flowers can be used in cakes, cookies, frozen desserts, candied, steeped in tea and brewed in coffee. They make a colorful garnish on fruit salads and sorbets.

- **Lavender** flowers taste more like lemon than lavender when used in small amounts. This is a delightful floral addition to puddings, ice creams, fruit dishes. It can also add to teas and other drinks.

- **Lemon blossoms** are a sheer delight. The flowers can be candied, and you can make lemon blossom sugar. The flower is even more distinctive in teas than the juice or the fruit. Lemon blossoms are a popular garnish for many mixed drinks in the Mediterranean basin. They're also used with tropical fruit salads.

- **Lemon Balm** is a popular herb with lemon scented foliage and pale pink flowers that impart a lemon flavor. These flowers make a great garnish in drinks, iced teas, fruit dishes, fish and frozen desserts. The flavor of the flowers is somewhat more intense than the leaves.

- **Lilacs** are the most delightful of the flowering shrubs. They give us color and fragrance, but there's more. The blossoms of the old fashioned lilac are a joy to the palate as well. Centuries ago lilac flowers were used as a breath freshener because they leave a clean, fragrant aftertaste. You can use the florets as a garnish on frozen desserts, as a flavoring in fruit dips, scones, cookies and pancakes.

- **Lotus** flowers and buds are a delicacy in China.

- **Marigolds** are one of my favorite edible flowers. The colors are great and the flavor is distinctive. Raw petals can be added to a salad. They can also be used to enhance the flavor of soups, stews, meat dishes. A friend of mine adds marigolds to vegetable juices and pasta sauces. The key with marigolds is to not overdo it. Too many flowers or petals can make any dish bitter.

28

- **Mexican tarragon** (Tagetes lucida) also called Spanish tarragon and root beer plant is a member of the marigold family. The cheerful yellow-orange flowers contain the same anise-like flavor as the leaves. This makes these flowers a perfect garnish on salads, iced teas, and chicken dishes. They can also be used in the preparation of soups, frozen desserts, cakes, cookies and syrups. This is another of the flowers that can be candied. Layering the flowers and granular sugar will produce a delightfully flavored sugar.

- **Mint** flower spikes are just as flavorful as the leaves and can be used in the same ways.

- **Nasturtiums** provide color and a tangy, almost peppery flavor to fine dining. Use in salads, as a garnish with meat dishes, as an ingredient in salad dressings and dips, or as a tasty addition to a baked potato.

- **Radish** flowers are white or cream colored with much the same taste as the root without the intensity. They make a great topping for a salad, can be added to soups, stews and meat dishes, or used as a topping on cooked vegetables or baked potatoes.

- **Roses** are "a delight to the eye as they pleaseth the nose" but that's only the beginning. The rose hips (the fruit) are a great source of vitamin C, and the flowers are valuable on the dinner table, too. The petals can be used in drinks, iced teas, hot teas, alcoholic beverages, and desserts. The unique flavor makes it a valuable garnish for salads, a tasty addition to cakes, cookies, custards and many other desserts.

- **Snapdragon** flowers make a colorful garnish.

- **Yucca** flowers and buds have an almost nutty flavor when cooked, fried or baked. To the Native Americans, this was a culinary staple.

Globe artichoke
29

Notes on Eating the Daisies and Other Flowers

- Please don't eat any flowers you are not able to positively identify and know are safe. Many flowers are poisonous, as are many leaves, fruits, and seeds.
- Educate children about what is edible and what isn't, just as you do with household chemicals, plants in the landscape, and other safety issues.
- Eat only flowers you know have been grown organically. The poisons contained in herbicides and insecticides are designed to kill. They can cause everything from mild discomfort to agony. In some cases, the cumulative effect can be deadly.
- Flowers don't last as long as fruits and vegetables. They are best harvested on the day they are going to be used.
- Flowers harvested in the morning are usually more flavorful and last longer.
- Harvested flowers can be stored in the refrigerator in a container filled with water or wrapped in moist paper towels for a day or two.
- Flowers, like all foods, are best consumed in moderation. Over-eating any food can cause some distress.
- Because many people have allergies, some may react to a given flower, while others do not. As an example: daisy and dandelion pollen can make some uncomfortable. A friend of mine is allergic to honeysuckle. It doesn't matter whether it's scenting the night air or gracing her iced tea, it still causes difficulty breathing.
- By using many of these flowers as seasonings, salt consumption can be reduced, while appetites are stimulated. They make a great addition to low fat and low sodium diets.
- Be careful not to mix too many floral flavors in one dish.

Chapter 4
A Sight to Behold

Beauty isn't only in the eye of the beholder. Beauty is something that affects all the senses. We hear the beauty of the breeze in the aspen or the bamboo grove. We inhale the beauty of lily-of-the-valley, a hemlock forest, a bouquet of roses. We feel the beauty of a waxy cactus flower, the fleshy leaves of an aloe, the velvet feel of an African violet's leaf, or the subtle beauty of birch bark. We taste the beauty of a sun-warmed tomato, a mint leaf or a fresh from the vine blackberry. But the fact remains that most of us view the beauty of a garden in terms of what we can see. We arrange our gardens for their visual impact, plan for the colors as the seasons change, attempt to overrule Mamma Nature and improve on her designs.

A garden doesn't have to provide visual stimulation in bold splashes of color, nor does it require so much micro-managing that it becomes a virtual reality bearing no resemblance to the real world.

A garden that is a thing of beauty to you may not be my choice. The beauty of the art of gardening is that the potential for expression is boundless. We can create a landscape that reflects color ranges, plant families, special habitats, or personal taste. In our greenscape we can create a comfort zone, set a mood, make a statement. The impact on our psyche may be dynamic with fountains and brilliant roses, or warmly subtle like a perennial border or shady fern nook with a comfortable bench. Perhaps your taste leans toward whimsy, a play garden for both children and adults.

One of the wonders of gardening is that, unless we are looking at a photograph of it, there is no way to make this only a visual experience. We can't walk through the garden without inhaling the smells of earth, moss, flowers, fruit and foliage. We hear the birds, the breezes, even wind chimes, along with the seasonal delight of frogs, squirrels, and bugs. We feel the subtle changes as we walk from the sunshine into the shade, step from lawn to path.

It's almost impossible to remain passive in a garden, because it bombards the senses.

The landscape doesn't have to be out there in the yard. The windowsill, a lighted plant stand, the porch, screen room, patio or deck can be a pleasing to the eye plantscape. Container gardening can be easy, efficient and fun.

Beauty is More Than the Plants

There is so much that helps to set the tone and mood, even in a small space, that goes far beyond the plants.

- **Walkways** and paths provide texture and color. This may be grass, brick, stone, gravel, bark chips or something original and unique that you have available. One gardener friend cast stepping stones of his own design. Into these he pressed assorted leaves and the footprints of each of his children.

- **Containers** and raised beds can add to the beauty of a garden by taking it from two dimensions to three. There is such a variety of container materials available today in assorted colors, styles and textures. These can make effective accents for your plants. Make certain when using containers that there are drainage holes. It's also wise to use a good quality potting soil, not the cheapest bag of black mud available. Simple clay pots can be painted for enhanced effect, or left to Mamma Nature's brush strokes of algae and patina.

- **Shade.** The path of the sun creates waves of shade, and the passage from sun to shade is also a thing of beauty. Plan for a place in the shade as well as opportunities to be warmed by the sun.

- **Furniture** is an important part of many gardens. Many operate under the misconception that it must be expensive and a work of art; however, the true beauty of furniture is in its comfort and convenience.

- **Ornaments.** Don't be shy about incorporating into the garden some statuary, whimsy, something to generate smiles. A friend of mine has statuary turtles throughout her landscape and patio garden. It becomes a quest of visitors to find them all.

- **Butterflies** are the bugs we all want in our gardens. We can plant invitations for them, but remember that the butterfly kids have the appetite of a teenager, so larval food plants will have to be grown, as well as nectar plants for the adults.

- **Arbors & trellises** add interest, dimension and visual impact. They can also cast needed shade, serve as a screen, and put flowers, foliage and fruit at eye level.

- **Light** is one of the overlooked aspects of the landscape, but without it we deny ourselves the use of the garden after sunset. There is a special and serene quality to the garden of the night. Some flowers are at their fragrant prime. We can see the moths dancing from flower to flower, delight in the appearance of fireflies, and look on the infinity of the universe. There is a special symphony of night sounds, and a boldness in the silhouettes of plant and tree.

Flowers for Color in the Garden of the Senses

Those living in the deep south know full well that color in the garden is a twelve month a year celebration. In Florida we have hibiscus, camellias and roses shouting their colors to the sun in the deepest, darkest months of winter. For those of us living and working in Michigan or Quebec, the colors of winter are gray and white.

Color is not only found in the bloom but in the buds, foliage, the bark, the seeds and seedpods. This gives us a wonderful opportunity to experience color outdoors whatever the season, wherever the location. The foliage of conifers like pine, spruce or hemlocks and broadleaf evergreens such as rhododendron, magnolia and bayberry give life to winter. So do the berries of dogwood, American beautyberry and bittersweet. The bark of the paperwhite birch and aspen glow in the grayness of winter, while cherry twigs, the silver of maple's bare branches, and the red of Osier dogwood and some willows season the snow with a dash of color.

Each season has its star bloomers, from the crocus and daffodils of early spring to the salvias, torenia and marigolds that make summer so alive. Autumn brings the colors of mums and the harvest.

The color of the blossoms attracts our attention, but so does the size and shape of the flower, the way the foliage compliments, accents or contrasts. A garden is a community and, like a community of people, it's most effective when there is healthy diversity. Even if that garden is on the windowsill. Much of the delightful color of the garden comes from the leaves. It may be a Colorado blue spruce or a Crimson King maple in the yard, or a colorful rex begonia among the ferns. The splash and dash of color draws our interest and pleases our artistic spirit.

Color in the Leaves of Autumn

- Aspen and cottonwood glow with an awesome golden display.
- Dogwood has red leaves and persistent red berries.
- Ginkgo gives us beautiful gold and tan leaves in autumn.
- Maples, red maple is a rainbow of color, sugar maple gives a rich blend of gold and tan while silver maple is pale yellow.
- Oaks add rich browns and some reds to the fall landscape.
- Persimmon displays its golden fruit as the brown leaves fall away.
- Redbud leaves are deep red and burgundy in the autumn.
- Sweet gum puts on a delightful burgundy show.

Colorful Indoor Foliage

Algerian ivy	Devil's backbone, pedalanthus
Aphelandra (zebra plant)	Dracena, varieties
Begonias	Epicias
Bromeliads	Fittonia
Caladiums	Geraniums, zonal
Calatheas	Strawberry geranium
Coleus	Swedish ivy
Cryptanthus	Pothos
English Ivy	Purple passion

Movement is also a thing of visual beauty

The flying flowers, those delightful creatures we call butterflies, and their nocturnal kin, the moths, give vitality to the garden. Ornamental grasses seductively sway their invitation to us to share the summer breezes. The dance of poplar leaves, even the nighttime folding of foliage in many of the legumes, is an act of sublime beauty to the eye. The dandelion seed taking wing toward its destiny, or the colorful autumn leaves on their final journey, are the sort of beauty that inspires poets. Who isn't awestruck when witnessing the opening of a night blooming cereus, or walking iris?

It's through movement that the garden becomes truly alive to the senses, and invites us to become a part of it. The growth of a leaf, the opening of a flower, the swelling of fruit are all movements as well, only the pace is different. Growth is the motion of life itself. Growth is the essence of our existence as well.

Butterfly on milkweed

Chapter 5
Hearing the Garden's Song

A friend of some years ago had lost her sight, and in doing so had made some great discoveries. She had been a gardener from early childhood and could not give up the simple joy of "playing in the dirt." She found that because she was less distracted by the visual kaleidoscope of the garden, she was able to hear it. She referred to the "symphony of a spring shower" where each plant became a musical instrument, played by the drops of rain.

Close your eyes and listen the harmony of the water striking the grass, leaves of the maple and needles of the pine. Listen to the drops falling through the leaves of a tree, ringing the wind chimes, tapping on the pots, the roof, the walk.

She could identify each bird that visited her yard, tell you what the squirrels were up to as they scampered through the oaks. Her musical "Four Seasons" included spring peepers and the scurrying of autumn leaves, summer's thunder and winter's snow drifted hush.

She purchased one of those little indoor fountains and put it in her living room. She added some splash stones, a large chunk of granite, a piece of hollow bamboo and some ferns. The sounds of the water falling from the granite over the bamboo and onto the stones she referred to as her "rock music."

We couldn't keep sound out of the garden, even if we wanted to. But there are many ways we can enhance our enjoyment of it.

• By eliminating the use of chemical pesticides, we can give the songbirds an opportunity to share our space.
• The sound of running water is as soul satisfying as it is stress soothing. We can use fountains, ponds with circulating pumps, and if space permits, we can enjoy a small brook or stream.

- Wind chimes can be effective if they aren't overdone. When there are too many, we run the risk of creating noise from music.
- An outdoor speaker or two can turn a gazebo or shady nook into a private retreat, or special place to entertain a guest, or enjoy some private time.
- Pausing long enough to listen is often all it takes.
- Don't forget one of childhood's favorite sounds, the delightful music of seeds in a dried gourd, or the rattle of beans in the pod.

A teacher friend played classical music in his greenhouse and insists that this makes seeds germinate quicker and encourages cuttings to root more readily. There have been numerous studies on music and plant growth, but most have been less than scientific. We do know a lot more about the effects of music on people. Regardless of the effect on the garden, we know music has a great influence on the gardener.

Chapter 6
In Touch with the Garden

One of the great advantages of being with plants, rather than just seeing pictures or looking at them from the other side of a fence, is that we can touch them. When sight is limited, we can employ our sense of touch to experience the garden. When we design sensory gardens for special populations, we include varieties of plants with distinctive or unique foliage, stems, flowers, fruit or bark. When we do plant shows and lectures, everyone has to touch the orchid cactus, bromeliads, amaranth flowers, bunny ears and so many others.

While we were doing a presentation to some Alzheimer's patients, one of them picked up a young dwarf pomegranate and began petting and stroking the leaves. The next time I glanced in that direction, two more patients and one nurse were doing likewise.

My two year old grandson, Alex, enjoys feeling the flowers and such botanical treasures as acorn caps and chestnut burrs. He thoroughly enjoys the feel of fall leaves, as well as the color. He's very sensitive to the difference in texture between varieties, and the difference between young leaves and mature ones.

Not only small children experience the garden with their fingers. Adults will press the velvet petals of a rose to their cheek, or rub with their fingers the coarse texture of a sunflower, a stalk of corn, or the waxen leaf of a water lily. There are few who can resist the delicate seedhead of that universal botanical toy, the dandelion. Unfortunately, many adults become timid with their years and literally lose touch with the living world. They wear gloves as insulation against reality, fear the chance appearance of a bug, and the possibility of getting dirt under fingernails. We become content to be virtual gardeners; or worse yet, garden voyeurs looking over the camera lens at someone else's joy. One couple who attended one of my 'garden chats' confessed that they didn't do any gardening themselves, because they could never get their plants to look as good as they look on HGTV. Does that really matter? The thrill is in the doing, the joy is in being a part of the life processes, of growth, not the pursuit of perfection.

A writer friend once commented that even in the consummate horticulture of Walt Disney World, the flowers wither or go to seed, the bedding plants complete their cycle and return to the soil, and even there they have failures. They have a staff second to none that plans, plants and maintains all that wonderful life. But that isn't your backyard or windowsill. Blessed indeed is the one who can reach out and feel the potted pineapple sage on the patio, or by hand harvest the row of beans in the garden, or touch the seasonal splendor of a dogwood tree, the buds, the flowers, the leaves and the bright red berries.

The true joy for the gardener comes in the contact. It's when we are willing to step out the door, pull off the gloves, feel the moist earth, hold in our hands the grains of life we call seeds, sense the vitality in a dormant twig, or connect with the wonder of the ultimate solar energy machine, a leaf.

I attended a conference that dealt with 'the handicapped' and came away with a new insight. One of the speakers said, "We are all handicapped, some by our past, some by our ignorance, all by our fears and insecurities." These few words so countered the tone of the conference which was . that we were noble because we chose to help *them*, the disabled, infirm, those with wounded psyche or mental limitations. These words put truth in perspective. It replaced the concept of *them and me* with a much more appropriate *us*. This replaced unneeded sympathy with valuable empathy. It made gardening a healing experience and an opportunity for growth together. It made crystal clear that both patient and professional were on a two way street. Both are capable of teaching, and both have the opportunity to learn.

Aristotle spoke of touch as the three-fold sense. He explained that this tactile sense told us hot-cold, hard-soft and rough-smooth. Two tiny little orbs control our ability to see, our sense of smell is limited to a small area inside the nose, we can hear because of the tiniest bones in the body, but we feel with the largest organ we possess, the skin. It should be noted that our sense of touch isn't limited to our fingertips or sensitive parts of our body, or even this external sack that keeps the rest of us in place. We feel with our mouth; that's part of the reason a baby puts everything in it. A child can determine all those qualities Aristotle mentioned with the tongue and tissues inside the mouth.

Pain is a response to too much touch, and serves as a warning to leave the stinging nettle alone, or be cautious of the fire ants, poison ivy or flames from the grill.

Some claim that the sense of touch is the most sensuous of senses. Many can identify plants by the feel of the leaf alone, the texture of the bark, but most of us rely on a multi-dimensional sensory exploration. This is one of the reasons that gardening can be such an emotional and spiritual experience, because it's a senso-round happening, it's life in 3-D.

Ornamental grasses for texture

Creating a "Feel Good Garden"

We can all enhance the opportunity for the tactile appreciation of our gardens, be they indoors or out. It's no sin to enjoy the beauty and bounty of the green world. It is, in fact, a gift for which we should be most appreciative.

- Plan and plant for a variety of textures.
- Remember that texture can be in the form of stem, bud, flower, fruit and seed as well as the leaf. Each plant can provide a multitude of varied stimuli.
- It isn't difficult to plant for varied textures each season, no matter where we live.
- Vegetation selected for its feel should be planted where it's easily accessible. Don't hide the "feel good" stuff behind fences or in the back of plantings.
- It isn't difficult to make your landscape, patio or even windowsill a multi-sensory experience. The feel of raspberries on the vine, amaryllis buds opening, mullein leaves, dried hops, strawflowers, petunia leaves, pampas grass and everything else that grows in our gardens is experienced by at least two or more of the senses. All we have to do is provide a variety of material.
- Non-plant material is an important part of tactile stimulation. The stone or wood of raised planters, the texture of containers, walkway material and mulches are a part of the garden we can reach out and touch.

Some Suggested Plants Pleasing to Our Sense of Touch

Hardy trees with interesting bark texture
- Birch trees with their paper smoothness
- Cherry bark has a warm and smooth texture
- Dogwood bark changes from twigs to trunk
- Hemlock bark is as alluring as the foliage
- Ironwood has a solid sinewy feel

- Oak bark has a ribbed quality to it
- Pine has a flaky bark with resilience
- Staghorn sumac has a fuzzy coating on the twigs
- Sycamore has the feel of two barks as it sheds from brown to white
- Walnut has the feel of deep determination
- White pine needles are easy to pet
- Winged euonymus, like corkbark elm, has a spongy texture

For a Touch of Green Indoors

African violet	Living stones, lithops
Camellia	Pineapple
Chrysanthemum	Purple passion
Coffee	Rex begonia
Cryptanthus	Rosary vine
English ivy	Sedum
Ferns	Stapilia
Hoya	String of pearls
Kalanchoe	Venus fly-trap
Jade crassula	Zygocactus (Christmas cactus)

Some Fruits, Seeds and Pods to Have and to Hold

Acorns and caps from burr oak
Berries of all kinds, raspberries, blueberries, strawberries
Chestnuts, both the nuts and the husks
Clover
Coneflower seedhead
Corn ears, husks, cobs, tassles, silk and stalks
Grains like oats, wheat, barley and rye
Grasses of all kinds
Lotus seedpods
Osage orange fruit
Peanuts and beanpods
Sycamore seed balls
Sweetgum burrs

Our sensations of touch, pain, temperature, pressure and vibration can be affected by medications, alcohol consumption, drugs, disease, dietary deficiencies and aging. Altered blood flow to the brain or to the touch receptors in the skin can alter our sense of touch and balance. If you have been sitting in an awkward position for some time, and then get up, you may find that your leg is 'asleep.' You can't properly feel the floor or ground beneath your feet. For many of the elderly, a similar inability to sense balance is chronic. This is one of the reasons walking is difficult and falls frequent.

As we age, our skin changes. It becomes thinner, and this can increase sensitivity to even light touch for many. For others, tactile sensation may decrease. Gardening gives everyone the opportunity to engage in rewarding activities at each individual's pace and within the confines of each person's abilities. Gardening gives us all an opportunity to experience our world, regardless of age or limitations.

Water lilies

Chapter 7
Beyond Our Physical Senses

Sense of Place

We live in the electronic and information age. More and more we have less and less contact with basic reality. Many of us today lead a virtual existence in a self imposed exile to the barren desert of office and apartment. It's no wonder that we live lives filled with stress, anger, frustration and depression as we struggle for our sense of place.

We feel that the world is spinning out of control, when the problem is one of excessive control. Our days are controlled to the minute because we have made ourselves slaves to a clock. We can't even escape the control a telephone has over us as we move from one place to another. We live in sterile cages and work in boxes and cubicles devoid of the stuff of life. We're afraid of the sun, afraid of water that isn't laced with chemicals, fear the air that isn't filtered, become terrified at the sight of an insect.

We eagerly seek a mythical life style depicted on TV and in the magazines. Our lust to control our environment precludes any opportunity to relax and experience it. By sharing our office and home with a few green and growing plants, we can begin to re-connect with our instinctive heritage. The Victorian age saw parlors filled with plants because they cleansed the air, dispelled melancholy, brought cheer and vitality into the home. In fact, they made the home comfortable.

Today we are fearful of the fungi that are a part of the web of life in the soil of home and office plants. Wouldn't it be better to rejoice in the air that has been cleansed, and the oxygen that has been provided by the plants in our homes and offices? As we enjoy sharing space with them, we can learn how to keep the soil healthy and avoid the fungus problems that can arise when a poor quality potting medium is kept too soggy.

When we bring plants into our existence we can no longer be passive. Gardening is a participation sport, and so is life itself. We become connected with something beyond us as we enter into this communion in the garden, as we play with plants and work at living. We can experience a sense of belonging, a sense of place in the universe, a sense that we are a part of something far greater than ourselves.

The art and act of gardening is, in the purest sense of the term, a spiritual journey that can help us all to find our sense of place.

A Sense of Comfort

As we get beyond the fear of our outdoor existence with its creepy-crawlies, weather that we can't control, and our fear of failure, we will be able to enjoy a feeling of contentment that is impossible when we assume that adversarial role. The gardener of the 21st century will be more a part of the garden, a part of nature. We will feel a lot better about working with our plants when we carry tools rather than weapons. Why do we celebrate the death of an insect more than the birth of a seed?

A sense of comfort will replace the sense of failure, the attitude of victimization. We have so long engaged in gardening as a competition that we came to thrill in the victory, not the gardening. How sad that we valued more the single rose in the same plastic bud vase as hundreds of others on the judges' table, and failed to see the beauty in the leaves, fallen petals, forming buds and even the defensive thorns that are a part of the whole.

The beauty of the garden isn't in the perfect plant, it's in the dynamics of life happening right there before our eyes. The joy isn't in a blue ribbon, it's in the sprouting of a seed, the unfolding of a leaf, the promise of a flower, the flavor of a harvest. My mother once commented, "You can't eat a blue ribbon, and you can't plant it next spring and grow more, either." There is comfort in being a part of the process.

Finding comfort in the garden doesn't mean that we get to sit there and watch the butterflies flutter by. Comfort isn't a lack of work, comfort is to be found in productive and satisfying labor. Much of our career work involves performing tasks for which there is no tangible accomplishment. In the garden we see the efforts bear results. The fact that we are purposefully expending energy, enough to make us sweat, is healthy for mind and body. Some people have no gardens; they are forced to go to gyms and exercise clubs where they pay big money for the opportunity to sweat. Gardeners can do this anytime they choose, with no membership fee. The butterflies are a bonus.

The important thing to remember here is that part of the comfort is derived from the fact that we are engaged in a partnership with Mamma Nature. The plants on our windowsill, deck or back forty all have an innate will to live, grow and produce a new generation. The plants we cultivate are powerful allies.

We are also comforted by our labors with the plants because we have a sense of presence. We are no longer standing outside the fence; we are fingers to fern frond, shoulder to tree trunk with life. We are in the garden, not watching it. In truth, we *are* a part of the garden.

Sense of Beauty

"Isn't this beautiful?" He spoke with such enthusiasm and conviction as he lifted the golden bell of a weed called sheep sorrel to my eyes. The minute flower is something most of us either trample or pull out by the roots as an unwanted intruder into our well manicured landscape. Errol's world extended as far as his wheelchair could take him, and at this stage in his life, that was from the windowsill in his room to the dining room at the end of the hall in this hospice facility. Errol was dying, and he knew it. Yet he could find the beauty in a weed that volunteered in a potted begonia on his windowsill.

We all have a sense of beauty, but many of us refuse to admit it, while others bury their instinctive opinion of what is beautiful under the opinions of the 'experts' in the field. The most primitive of our ancestors knew, appreciated and created beauty. The difference is that they valued their own talents so highly that they all viewed themselves as both artist and critic. In today's culture we have advanced to the point where insecurities so rule us that we employ others to create art for us. Then we hire experts to tell us what we like.

In the garden, experts tell us what to grow, what the prettiest flowers are, and how we should arrange them. Why? Why are we so willing to accept the opinions, attitudes and advice of others instead of following our own sense of beauty? The garden, even if it is limited to a begonia on a windowsill, is a place for you not only to cultivate your plants, but your sense of beauty as well. We all need beauty in our lives. We all expend great energy and resources in the pursuit of beauty. The greatest art isn't the Mattise or Renoir in the museum, it's the watercolor you did in your backyard, or the crayon art proudly presented by a first grader as an expression of the joy of creating and giving beauty. It can also be the perennial border, the strawberry bed, the apple tree or the ivy covered wall. The beauty that we see is not only in the eye of the beholder, the beauty is the beholder.

In the garden, we feel we have a hand in creating the beauty. We are connected with other life and the forces of nature. We can influence the creation, be a part of it, but we don't truly own it or control it. The wonderful aspect of this is that spiritually, if we are a part of the garden, we are a part of the beauty found there. In fact this makes each one of us beautiful in our own existence. This is something Errol taught me, while I was giving him horticultural therapy.

The beauty of the garden isn't limited to the flowers found there, or the butterflies that visit, or the produce harvested. There is also the beauty of activity to be found there. Beauty may be seen, heard, felt, tasted or inhaled. The depth of our appreciation is limited only by our willingness to experience. The beauty of the art of gardening is in the involvement of body, mind and spirit.

A Sense of Being

Perhaps the most important of our senses is the sense of being. A sense of well-being grows from this, and it grows well in our gardens. The first five of the senses discussed above: smell, taste, sight, hearing and touch give us clues as to how we can interpret our environment. They instinctively warn of danger, tell us when we are approaching food, shelter, and beauty; the basic information we need for our physical existence.

They also enable us to appreciate and understand the world around us. These senses make it possible for us to experience joy, sorrow, pleasure and pain. They work best when they can function in cooperation with each other. To see, feel and smell the rose is a far more rewarding experience than merely looking at a picture of one, or sniffing a bottle of rose perfume. This combination of sensual experiences is an instinctive need. Yet many of us are denied the use of one or more of these dimensions. In the garden the sensory limitations can be compensated for by the natural communion with life, and new perspectives and awareness can be discovered.

Many of us don't have physical sensory limitations. We aren't blind or deaf. Our bodies haven't forgotten how to smell, taste or feel. But we have. We have replaced the thrill of discovery with the fear of the unknown, the joy of challenge with the fear of failure, the natural world with a sterile prison. We feel trapped in our everyday life, because that's exactly what we are. To compensate, we try to satisfy our instincts with artificial stimuli. We may be able to fool our body, we can even trick our mind into thinking we are happy at times, but in the deepest part of our being, in our very soul, we know something is lacking. This is our instinctive connection with the variety of life. Our instinctive need is to be a part of it, not just a spectator.

Peaceful setting

PART TWO
GARDENING AS THERAPY

The last chapter discussed things we don't often think of as senses, because our temptation is to limit sensation to the physical. But the physical part of our being doesn't exist independent from the mind, the emotions or the spirit.

In a conversation with some adult education students, the comment was made that it was fascinating how each plant and animal had a role to play in the eco-system that we call our backyard. This student spoke as an outsider, failing to comprehend the vital role she also played in the system. It never dawned on her that this was her eco-system, too.

Now, let's take this concept of the inter-dependency of the symbiotic web of life one step further. We need to look inward. We are all physical entities with physical needs. We are also mental entities, and we use this mental self to interpret what the physical self experiences. In the web of self, there is also an emotional existence that dictates our response to the mental interpretation. In the center of our web of self, at the epi-center of our existence is the spirit, the soul of what we are. This spiritual self also needs to be nourished.

When sudden trauma, accumulated stress, or a lifetime spent learning the wrong lessons wounds the spirit, the mind and the body suffer too. This is why bad stress leads to cancer, heart attacks, ulcers and other physical infirmities. This is why anger and violence are the illegitimate twins of hopelessness and despair.

We speak of depression resulting from a sense that we can't control our life, but don't you think it might be more likely that it's the natural response to broken connections? Control is a heavy burden to carry, whether your are the one being controlled, or the one controlling. The drive to be in control is in itself an overwhelming stress. A sense of being connected lightens the emotional load for all concerned, and permits the smothered soul space to breath.

We don't exist in a vacuum. In fact, we can't, because our minds won't let us. Our sense of being is linked to all the other threads in our web of self, but our web of self is only a thread in the universal existence of all life. We are a part of something far greater than we can comprehend, if only we permit ourselves the opportunity to accept the connections. If we can do this, then the web of life, our ecosystem, becomes our safety net.

During a presentation at an elementary school, I asked the students who lives in the garden. I expected answers like butterflies, ladybugs, toads, birds and chipmunks, but perhaps one little boy came closer to the truth than we know when he said, "God lives in my Dad's garden."

I thought this was a great answer and asked for an explanation. He gave it.

"When Dad goes out there the first thing he says is, 'My God, look at all those weeds.'"

Chicken soup may well be good for the soul, but a few vegetables from the garden can make it taste better. We can come out of our self imposed exile in the synthetic desert and feed the soul in the garden.

Not all stress is bad, and no garden is stress free. However, we often create our own stress because we have become so accustomed to pressure and worry that if our load is lightened, we miss it. This is as foolish as missing a toothache. One of the simple facts of life is that pain, suffering and stress are a part of our existence. But then, so are pleasure, joy and contentment. The key is in keeping all of these in balance. In fact the secret formula for a happy life, as well as the recipe for successful gardening, is in the simple word *balance.*

Some of us discover that stress and pressure take on a life of their own and grow like weeds. We make our lives so complicated that we never have time to live, or we fill our mind with so many fears that we lack the courage to really live. This is where gardening as therapy enters the picture.

Chapter 8
The Therapeutic Garden

The *Random House College Dictionary* defines therapy thus.

Therapy 1. The treatment of a disease or other disorder, as by some remedial or curative process. **2.** A curative power or quality. **3.** Physical treatment for curing or rehabilitating a patient or to overcome a physical defect, as by exercise, etc. **4.** Treatment of the psychologically or socially maladjusted....

In this section of this book we are going to look at how gardening can be a therapeutic experience for each of us. This is the basis for a profession called horticultural therapy. While much of the emphasis in the field of HT is on special populations and individuals with limitations and disabilities, each and every one of us can gain from the connections working with plants provides. Whether we want to admit it or not, we all need therapy.

What Is Horticultural Therapy?

It's simply gardening as therapy. Horticultural therapy is a process utilizing plants and horticultural activities to improve the social, educational, psychological and physical adjustment of persons, thus improving their body, mind and spirit.

The garden is a safe place, a benevolent setting where everyone is welcome. Plants are non-judgmental, non-threatening and non-discriminating. Plants have a life of their own, but do respond to the care given. Plants don't care what color we are, whether we have been to kindergarten or graduate school, whether we are poor or rich, healthy or infirm, a victim of abuse or an abuser, handicapped or blind, addicted or depressed. Our plants don't care if we can call them by name, or only caress them with arthritic hands.

We all suffer from the burdens and stress our everyday lifestyle heaps upon us. Time actively spent gardening can be a source of relaxation and escape. However, it can be much more than that. It can be a source of renewal. We can make compost of these emotional and psychological burdens, and grow a stronger self. A part of this regeneration comes from the simple fact that in the garden there are always discoveries to be made.

One of the most therapeutic activities we can do is so simple and so good for both us and the plants we are cultivating. Simply walk through the garden every day; look over the botanical treasures on your windowsill or patio. You'll discover which ones need water or what bugs are uninvited dinner guests. But better than the problems to be solved, are the discoveries to be made. A flower bud opens. A seed germinates. Leaves unfurl. A vine hugs its support. Fruit begins to blush with ripeness. The seasons mark their passage. These are the discoveries of life; the threads of our connection; the therapy for our soul.

For those of us going through the trauma of life change (job loss, divorce, death of a loved one, etc.) gardening can be a comfort and a retreat, a respite and a renewal. It can be a way of dealing with grief. A friend of mine, Elan Miavitz, developed a grief garden program that can be employed by hospice organizations to help family members accept loss and work through the grief process.

Often, those of us who experience a loss find our self-confidence shattered. A garden is a safe place to heal, a place where we make successes great and small, a place where we find that we do make a difference. We can literally grow self-esteem in the garden.

Not only does the beauty and variety of life found in a communion with plants soothe the stresses we live with, this activity also gives the gift of hope and a reason for tomorrow. After all, gardeners must have unlimited optimism and faith to plant a dried up tuber and see a dahlia, or specks of dust and see begonias, or look out on winter bare branches and taste the apples.

Chapter 9
Therapy for the Body

"Old Mike" is what everyone called him. He was a steelworker from the old country who spoke a curious blend of Italian and English. The mill was his job, but his joy was the garden. Before his shift began he would spend time tending the tomatoes, squash, beautiful pole beans and magnificent cabbages. When he got home, if there was sufficient daylight he would return to his terraced hillside of garden beds.

One thing the neighbors would tell you about Old Mike was that he always whistled while he was weeding, hoeing, trimming, feeding, watering, planting and harvesting. As each crop matured, the harvest was divided into bags and boxes and shared with the neighbors. That was the case until that terrible day in July when Old Mike didn't come home from work. This little old man with the great, kind and generous heart was in the hospital.

The coronary incident occurred shortly after lunch. The recovery was slow, but he came home eventually. The doctors gave his wife strict orders to keep him quiet and still. They told her gardening in the summer heat was out of the question.

He would sit at the kitchen table and look out at the hillside garden, at the yellowing squash leaves, at the weeds now overshadowing the carrots and cabbages, at the tomato vines that needed to be tied up and pinched back. He would sit and weep, but his wife insisted that he follow the doctor's orders.

That was until one morning when she left the house to do the grocery shopping. No sooner was she out the driveway, than Old Mike was out the kitchen door. He knew his limitations, but he sat and pulled weeds, picked a few tomatoes and a basket of zucchini and patty-pan squash. He had weeded an area about the size of the kitchen when she returned. While she scolded and repeated all the dire warnings from the doctors, he simply smiled and ate one of the sun warmed tomatoes.

Some mornings he would steal an hour in the garden before she arose. Any time she visited with the Cicarelli's or Mrs. Polanchek, he would slip out the back door and trim, weed and water. Every time she would return and scold him, but that, too, became a part of the game. Soon the garden was returned to its former glory, and Old Mike was making a strong comeback as well.

By mid September he was pulling his grandson's wooden wagon up and down the street as he shared bags of vegetables and the grapes that were now at their prime. Old Mike was back.

He was able to return to work in December, although the doctors had told him he would never work again. It was five years later when he finally retired from the mill and expanded the garden. He continued to share the bounty with the neighborhood until he was eighty-nine. That's horticultural therapy. That's what it's all about.

Why Gardening Is Good for the Body

If you're reading this book, the odds are that you're already gardening, so you might want to use the following notes to help someone else reap the physical benefits.

- The labor expended in the garden is self-paced exercise. Plants are patient. They don't ask you to move swiftly, meet production quotas or punch a time clock.
- For many of us, the workplace doesn't give us the opportunity to use many of our muscles. The garden is an open air health spa, a gym without membership fees.
- Gardening is great exercise for arthritic hands and joints.
- Both gross and small muscle coordination benefit from these simple repetitive exercises.
- Because we can move at a pace that is comfortable, we can reduce the stress of exercising.
- The bending, reaching and stretching that the average landscape requires is great for our circulatory system, too.
- Stress carried within us can so poison the body that it falls victim to everything from colitis to cancer. Much of this stress can be discarded in the gardening.
- We can engage in this therapeutic activity at the time of our choosing. We don't have to make appointments, drive through traffic to get there, or wait in line to play in our own backyard.

Hummingbird & honeysuckle

Gardeners live longer

Over eighty percent of all Americans who have reached the century mark have spent a major portion of their lives in the garden.

There may be several reasons for this. The most obvious is that folks that are tending vegetable gardens probably have a healthier diet. The exercise helps to condition the body and keep all systems working. But there may be something more to it than this.

People take a deep breath, use the oxygen inhaled, then exhale carbon dioxide. Plants don't breath like we do, but they take air into their system through openings in the leaves called stomata. They use carbon dioxide and discard oxygen. Isn't this a great system? You'd almost think we were designed to work together, wouldn't you?

One full grown oak tree produces enough oxygen each day to supply the needs of one adult, and enough leaves each fall to provide healthy exercise for that same adult.

Stale air makes people tired, impairs their ability to concentrate, causes headaches, lethargy and irritability. A few plants around the office can increase both morale and productivity. A few green and growing plants in the home through long northern winters can also have a positive effect on the body and attitude.

The fact that plants provide an oxygen enriched atmosphere is one reason why they were placed in homes, sickrooms and hospitals a century ago.

There's also another benefit that's often overlooked, although NASA has studied the use of plants for this purpose. Plants literally filter the air we breath. They remove, process or trap many airborne pollutants. Their studies suggest that two or three plants per 100 square feet of floor space will serve as effective natural pollution filters.

A series of university studies discovered that much of the formaldehyde in a room (released from paneling, particle board, insulation, carpet, even clothing) was absorbed into the leaves of many common foliage plants, where it was transformed into sugars used by the plant to produce new growth or released into the atmosphere as oxygen. Ficus leaves removed and broke down nicotine, while pothos plants removed it from the air and stored it in their leaves.

Not only are plants valuable air purifiers in the home, they serve the same purpose in the workplace. There have been some concerns about dangerous molds that might grow in the soil of potted plants. Some places have foolishly removed the plants when it would have been far wiser to make the soil healthy and continue to reap the physical and psychological benefits of working among living plants.

First, we have to understand that soil itself isn't just a pile of dirt and chemicals, it's a community of organisms. Many plants require the presence of these fungi and other microorganisms to transform the elements and minerals in the soil into compounds that can be absorbed by the roots. These organisms help to break down the organic matter in the soil into useful materials, maintain proper levels of moisture and air in the soil, and also defend against soilborne diseases. Healthy soil is no problem for most of us.

Keeping the Soil Healthy

1. Start with a premium quality potting soil, not the budget brand. Good soil doesn't form adobe bricks when it dries out. In fact, good soil is loose and almost fluffy, with a healthy earthy smell to it.

2. Use a container with drainage holes. Healthy soil must contain a large percentage of air. If the soil begins to look and smell like the black swamp, it's not going to be a good environment for your carefully chosen plants.

3. A saucer under the pot will protect the desk, table or floor, but potted plants shouldn't sit in saucers full of water. This saturates the soil and encourages diseases that rot out roots and stems.

4. The best practice is to water the plant well, let it sit for approximately half an hour, then dump whatever collects in the saucer.

5. Wick watering systems take much of the guess work out of watering, as they naturally maintain a healthy moisture level.

There are many soilless growing mediums on the market, and several systems that grow plants in fertilizer enriched water. While this is somewhat like feeding our pet philodendron intravenously, it does work for those among us with serious allergies.

Part of the increase in respiratory illness and asthma is attributed to the fact that we live and work in closed in buildings where the natural dispersal of pollutants can't take place. Air conditioning and filters are effective at removing dust, but they cannot trap the vapors that cause problems. A green leaf may well be a more efficient solution to this problem. Many claim that the "sick building syndrome" can be cured by simply placing more live plants in the living and working space. While this may not be the total solution, it does seem to help.

The following plants grow well in the average home or office and actively reduce air pollution.

Spider plant
Golden pothos
Peace lily
English ivy
Chrysanthemum
Corn plant and other Dracena varieties
Weeping fig *Ficus benjamina*
Rubber tree *Ficus elastica*
Fiddle leaf fig *Ficus lyrata*
Philodendron

While these all proved effective in filtering formaldehyde, benzene and trichloroethylene out of the air we breathe, this shouldn't discourage us from using other plants, as well. Ferns, palms, cast iron plants, poinsettias, diffenbachia and most of the other common house plants also make good air filters while they add oxygen to the air we breath. The top ten were partly chosen for their durability and willingness to accept less than ideal light conditions.

If you want to pursue this subject further, Dr. Bill Wolverton's book *How to Grow Fresh Air: 50 Houseplants that Purify Your Home or Office* is a great place to start. Another good source of information is the Plants for Clean Air Council at 3458 Godspeed Road, Davidsonville, MD 21035, phone (410) 956-9036.

In physical therapy the body is trained, or re-trained, in how to function. Muscles, including the heart, learn to expand their limits. Physical therapy helps individuals gain strength, coordination and endurance. We learn how to breath more effectively, thus taking in more oxygen and removing more of the waste air. This improves circulation and stimulates the brain. All the reaching, bending and stretching that tending the garden requires are a part of normal physical and occupational therapy programs. In many cases where an individual is recovering from surgery, an accident or stroke the gardening experience can give purpose to what otherwise can be painful exercise.

Occupational therapy is designed to help people adapt to their limitations by reaching their full physical and mental potential through meaningful activity. The flaw in our concept of these therapies is that they are only for individuals with disabilities. We can all profit from a therapy program that meets our needs and invites us to reach just a little further. Gardening is one of the ways this can be achieved.

It's also important to note that this therapy for the body isn't practiced in isolation. One psychologist encourages her patients with eating disorders to spend as much time as possible gardening. She insists that the physical exercise tones the muscles and increases the metabolism, but these are secondary. The real advantage is psychological. When we feel that we have accomplished something, when we surround ourselves with beauty, we feel better about ourselves. She insists that it's impossible to treat the body without treating the mind and the spirit. One of my students perhaps said it best when she commented, "When I bury all my anger in the flowerbeds, I can turn it into something beautiful myself."

The essence of horticulture is action. The gardener is actively engaged with not only the plants but the environment. The gardener encourages, nurtures, defends and creates. There should be no such thing as a stress-free garden nor a place in the garden for a lazy gardener. As one of my students who was recovering from a stroke commented, "I have so much to do out there [pointing toward the arboretum where she volunteered], there's just no time left to fret about it."

The physical exercise of gardening is good for us. We stretch the muscles when we hoe and weed. We water the landscape with a little of our sweat, and breathe better for it. We exercise our senses and sleep sounder. All this because we re-connected with our instinctive roots.

Chapter 10
Therapy for the Mind

The human mind is so complex, so powerful, yet so fragile a marvel. Without the mind the body has no direction, the emotions have no meaning, and the spirit is without expression. Unfortunately, with a machine this complicated there are a multitude of things that can go wrong. It takes a little effort on our part to keep this wonder of creation functioning well.

Simply living in our contemporary society is stress overload, both physically and mentally. These stresses take a toll on us in so many ways. We become nervous eaters, we drink too much, we smoke, we become angry. These are the obvious manifestations, but there are others. As our ability to concentrate diminishes, the attention span becomes shorter and shorter, we lose the ability to follow directions and solve problems. Even our basic communication skills suffer. But perhaps the greatest sacrifice we make to stress is that we lose our ability to cope. Then we either become aggressive or depressed.

Depression robs us of our willingness and ability to be ourselves. Depression isn't something that we can simply "get over." It's probably the most misunderstood illness. It revolves around a loss of our sense of place and purpose. Many argue that it's all a matter of control, but for most it's more a matter of losing connection, of being out of harmony, of drifting without purpose.

Aggression and anger are ways we tell the world we can't take anymore. When we shout, curse or strike out, we're saying that we're no longer in control, either of the situation or ourselves. Often we transfer the anger to someone or something that we can control or dominate. This can be in the form of verbal or physical abuse, road rage or target practice. It's better to find acceptable outlets for this anger than to bury it all inside us. One of the most socially acceptable ways to vent these feelings is by hoeing, weeding or pruning; even mowing the grass can provide an outlet.

Frustration with work, finances, family or relationships can also rob us of our mental potential and interfere with our

63

ability to enjoy life. Like anger, frustration is a poison to the mind and body. Avoiding frustration could be one of the benefits of growing plants in the workplace. We find comfort in the transplanted jungle of growth, vitality, and life. In the 21st century, there will be gardening opportunities where we work. Office buildings may well have garden clubs as a means of relaxing, socializing and reducing the stress levels. As we move from competition to cooperation as a life concept, we'll have to do things like this to relearn the meaning of concepts like trust, friendship, community and acceptance.

Schools and communities are already discovering the value in shared gardening as a source of pride, confidence and sense of belonging. Inner city neighborhoods have cleaned up vacant lots that were littered with garbage, broken liquor bottles and rats. Together, they turned them into oases of life, a source of beauty and pride. In these areas the sense of hopelessness is replaced with optimism, fear gives way to joy as, not only the work, but the fruits of the community's labor are shared. We are all capable of learning how to shake hands instead of fists.

Sunflower

George had worked hard all his life, and was proud of the fact that he had "earned his keep." Even after retiring he continued to work part-time and put in some volunteer hours. Then his wife took ill. Soon after she passed away, his health began to fail. His children insisted that he sell the house he could no longer care for and enter a local nursing home. He obediently did as his children wished, but it was a difficult transition. There was too much to adjust to, so many losses in too short a time. The depression became more and more profound. Many days he did little more than stare out the window of what he referred to as his cell.

One day, as he stood at the window thinking about the happier times he had known and mourning their loss, he noticed that the flower beds outside were dry. The plants were critically wilted. He slipped outside and found the hose. After he watered that bed, he discovered several other areas of the landscape that were suffering as well.

They caught him and led him back to his room with stern scoldings and mutterings about the onset of dementia. Fortunately one of the CNA's understood. She came to work an hour early the next morning and met with the director of nursing. Reluctantly the DON agreed that she could take George out on her off duty time and work in the landscape, as long as he didn't handle any dangerous tools. Soon two other residents joined them in watering, trimming, weeding and enjoying the contact with green and growing life.

George had a reason to look out the window now. The landscape never looked as good as it did after the "garden club" began taking an active role in its care. And they had a reason to get up in the morning, they formed friendships, and they felt they had a purpose in life.

Donnisa had the pressure of a career that demanded too much time pretending to be someone she wasn't. She didn't enjoy retail management, the hours, the petty problems, the unreasonable demands and impossible goals from the home office. To the career pressure was added the burden of a teenaged daughter on drugs and a husband whose job took him away from home for days and weeks at a time. Home was a battle field and work was a war zone. Donnisa felt trapped, without a safe place to rest, recover and renew. She found her patience exhausted, the future dark. Every phone call was a problem, every memo a conflict to be resolved. Her ability to concentrate declined, her memory became faulty, she made frequent mistakes, was short tempered with staff and impatient with herself.

Like many of us, she was also suffering from sensory overload. The symphony of life was a dissonant cacophony of phones, faxes, advertising sound bites and dozens of voices all talking at once. The crescendo of stresses climaxed with a scream for help in the form of a suicide attempt. That got her a ticket to the local locked unit.

There, in the relative quiet, she discovered the calm beauty of a garden. The fragrance of the flowers and herbs, the colors and textures brought her to a place she had never been, but she instinctively knew existed. The institution had a horticultural therapist on staff who introduced her to the fine art of gardening. These skills she took home with her, not because they solved all her problems, not because it covered up the life threatening stress, but because it gave her a way to cope, a reason for tomorrow.

She found that when she set aside time for herself, time to tend the patio garden she created at her apartment she was able to, for a short time, do something just for herself. Soon the patio wasn't big enough. She learned how to say NO to the time demands of her job when she began to volunteer at a local botanical garden.

There are a number of mental and emotional benefits derived from working with plants. One doesn't have to be institutionalized to reap these rewards, either. We don't live in isolation. We live in families, communities and work forces. Our instincts require that we be a part of such social structures, but our instincts also long for interaction with, not just other people, but plants and animals, too. Somewhere in the deepest recesses of the mind is a need for the security an open forest provides, the adventure of a winding path, the beauty of life, the shelter of trees, the food from the roots and fruits. These are all ways the green world sustains us. When we imprison ourselves in a virtual world with synthetic air, synthetic plants, remotely prepared food and "no pets allowed" we deny our instincts. We exile ourselves to the most barren of deserts.

Gardening as a Means of Connecting with Life

We can't separate the physical and mental aspects of our existence. Again, the purists talk about therapy in terms of people with disabilities. The person confined to a wheelchair definitely profits from being able to cultivate and provide care for another living organism. Children and adults with mental disabilities or limitations gain a sense of accomplishment. They also make cognitive connections between their actions and the results of what they do. There's something calming, empowering and reassuring about being a part of the growth process. The plants become metaphor for self. This isn't true only of those profoundly disabled, it's true for all of us. What often begins as an escape from something soon becomes the journey, a goal in itself.

None of us can separate our biological self from our psychological self. Nor should we try. Yet the work place sometimes demands that unnatural division of ourselves. Being a spectator at life also separates us from ourselves. In the garden we are freed to integrate the mind, the body and the spirit; we can function as a whole. We also do this when we make music, when we do art, and when we allow ourselves to be creative. Once we can connect with ourselves we are better able to become the social animal our instincts call for us to be. By stepping into the garden, by removing ourselves from the part of our existence that is the source of our tension, we prepare ourselves to face tomorrow with courage, confidence and acceptance. This integration of self is sometimes called harmony, sometimes peace. Whatever we chose to call this phenomenon, it's a gateway to survival.

We don't have to be handicapped to benefit from the therapy harvested from flower and leaf.

All work is a Substitute for the Hunt and Harvest

Our ancestors, back in the days before the wheel, iron weapons, city states, and what we think of as civilization, spent a few hours each day gathering the needs for survival. Today, we work two jobs and still live on borrowed money to almost make ends meet. The work of the family, clan or tribe was hunting and gathering, not just meat and wild parsnips, but shelter, safety and beauty. Everyone worked together toward these common goals. Cooperation was the instinct that dominated, not personal greed. Everyone had a direct connection to both the hunt and the harvest. Today we work at a job that often presents us with no tangible sense of accomplishment. The reward for our labors isn't a handful of fresh berries, or a dye that we can paint with, it's a paycheck that only symbolizes the reward for the work we never saw accomplished. We are all out of connection with our instincts. We are frustrated by a sense that our efforts have not been productive.

After we have become conditioned to fear real life, the instinctual sense of failure leads us to a frenzy of acquiring. Going shopping is the only harvest we permit ourselves, but it never satisfies. We always have an empty feeling after the Christmas presents have all been opened. We have the sense that something is missing. Our instinctive need for the connection remains unsated. We don't sense fulfillment because we only vicariously knew the hunt and harvest. We didn't truly experience it ourselves.

In the garden we engage the life forces, we face the risk of failure, yet retain the ability to influence. We may only harvest a tomato, or a fistful of flowers, but in that, we harvested ourselves. We are what we seek in the garden, we are what we grow there, we are what we gather there.

68

For those of us who are retired or out of the work force, there is often a lack of identity. We feel that we no longer contribute to society. The garden gives us purpose, whether we are growing dinner or the flowers to grace the table. In the garden we earn our keep. There is a dependency from the plants. This means we have responsibility to them. In a study done in a nursing home, one group of residents was given the freedom to select the plants and care for them themselves. A second group had the same number of plants in their rooms, but that greenery had been selected and cared for by staff. The first group showed significant improvement in alertness and general sense of well being. They were actively involved with their environment.

Gardening is a Creative Exercise

Plants themselves are a lesson in creativity. When we sow a seed, strike a cutting, plant a bulb or tuber we become involved in a creative partnership with the forces of nature. The sense of accomplishing something positive, something beautiful or functional, is what creativity is about. We see the measured growth in the plant; without realizing it, we are also experiencing the growth in ourselves. When we do floral arranging with our own flowers, create a bonsai from a juniper runt, a topiary from a wandering ivy, a landscape from a naked lawn, a meal from our own produce, root a cutting, or coax a plant into bloom we know the thrill and joy of creative expression. For those among us who have known abuse, or have been abusers ourselves, the sense of creative fulfillment, of productive creativity is one step in reclaiming ourselves.

Every Garden Has Its Weeds

One of the lessons we learn as we kneel in the garden is that life isn't always easy. Sometimes there are bugs and weeds. Sometimes thirst isn't satisfied, nor is hunger. Both plants and people need to feel the warm sun, but both must

69

survive the storms and the dark nights. In the garden we learn to accept failure, deal with frustration and face the problems that accompany our everyday life. We learn that in every life things will go wrong, no matter how carefully we prepare. Sometimes we have to simply tolerate inconvenience and accept occasional failure, while we work and plan for tomorrow. Working with plants gives us an opportunity to safely fail as well as succeed. We learn that nature isn't perfect, nor do we need to be, nor can we be.

Weeding the garden is an active therapeutic experience, whether it's the literal garden or an allegory for our lifestyle. But gardening is much more than weeding and defending against insects, just as life is more than vigilance and battle. Life in the garden is a symbiotic relationship, and we are a part of it. We can't kill all the bugs if we expect to see the butterflies, or eat the honey or the apples if we chase the bees away. We can't poison the soil and expect the plants to grow. We can't force the flowers to bloom, we can only encourage them. In the garden we learn about our limitations as well as our potentials.

You Deserve a Break Today

Gardening is a source of fascination that commands our attention. We easily become involved in the wonder of it all as the work and communion absorb us. This intense concentration is of great advantage when we are trying to train people with attention deficit disorders, or individuals who need to learn how to function independently. But the value isn't limited to those with cognitive or developmental difficulties. For all of us, it's a break from the pressure of phones and family, work demands and the pressure to produce. Gardeners get a break from the constant stress, the normal tension that's a part of everyday existence.

Several major corporations are now bringing live plants into the work space, some are even providing "garden time" where workers can vent the anger on the weeds, escape the stress for a few refreshing minutes, and find promise in the growth. The future will see workplace garden clubs as well as the workout room. It certainly beats a padded cell.

Growing Social Skills in the Garden

Working as a part of a team teaches compromise. We learn how to share as we work toward a common goal. The garden in a school, work or community setting provides opportunities for social interaction, communication and cooperation. In horticultural therapy programs in prisons, drug and alcohol rehab centers and in homeless shelters, these social skills are developed through active participation, sometimes voluntary, sometimes not.

Steve was the father of a twelve year old the school had labeled "at risk." One afternoon while Steve was at the school meeting with the principal for the eleventh time that year, he noticed something at the back of the school grounds. It was a shade house, with stacks of empty pots and a weed covered pile of topsoil. He was told it was left over from a remodeling program about six years ago. As he left he saw several students throwing candy wrappers and drink containers into the landscape. He watched in shocked silence as they walked over the junipers and marigolds that were struggling to survive in the beds at the entrance. He didn't understand why these kids didn't have any pride in their school, or themselves.

That evening, after supper, Steve and his "at risk" son were doing a little yard work when one of his school friends came over and began to help with the trimming and watering. They were joking and laughing. Talk ranged from sports to cars and girls, but what struck Steve was that they both seemed to be enjoying what they were doing. They were being productive.

While the two boys put the tools away, Steve prepared a snack of nachos and salsa and some soft drinks. As they sat on the back porch, he began to ask questions about the shade house at the school and why the kids abused the landscape and littered their own school grounds. Gradually, an idea was taking form.

The next few weeks saw Steve at the school almost as much as his son. First he made the proposal to the principal, who was skeptical but willing to give it a try if the school board would approve. At the school board meeting the next month, Steve made his proposal and after a little discussion about insurance liability and expense, they gave him the green light to try his experiment. That's the way The John F. Kennedy Middle School Garden Club started.

He called together a team that included the science teacher, several students, a local horticultural therapist and the master gardeners from the agricultural extension office. After a couple planning sessions, they talked to the rest of the students about what the club would do. Steve's plan was simple. First they would clean up the school grounds. Next, they would repair the shade house and cover it with plastic as a temporary greenhouse. Then they would begin to grow more shrubs and plants for the as yet unnamed school beautification project.

There were dire warnings from other faculty and the maintenance staff, but the kids were coming forward with ideas of their own. Several went to local garden centers and got donations of plant material. They designed posters that went in the hallways. The goal soon became "JFK Middle School, the coolest school in Russell City." The students began to police the landscape and littering became a thing of the past. Students were coming to school early to get watering done or check on their seedlings.

What began as a program for about a dozen at risk students soon involved fifty-three enthusiastic kids learning to cooperate and work together toward a common goal. The next year they were taking hanging baskets and dish gardens to local nursing homes, were planning a vegetable garden for a local food bank and talking about making a butterfly garden.

We all benefit from the active involvement in the garden. We can value the time alone with our plants. The exercise is good for our bodies and minds. But there are social advantages too. We can all experience social growth when we share garden space with a friend. Not only do we find therapy for our jangled nerves and tense bodies, but we have the opportunity to be a therapist for others. We can share plants with a neighbor, take a group of friends, co-workers, even family on a field trip to a local botanical garden. Take classes and attend workshops. Share the joy.

Garden harvest

Chapter 11
Therapy for the Soul

Being with plants provides a sense of place in the universe, communion with nature, a sense of peace and harmony. While it's satisfying to the body when we sweat and stretch the little used muscles during the grunt work of gardening, not all time spent with our plants needs to be physically active. While we exercise the mind in a multitude of ways when we work and play with the backyard landscape, some of the most valuable benefit comes from just being there.

At least a portion of the stress that burdens us today is from the self imposed need to be perpetually engaged. Much of the value in professional horticultural therapy programs comes after the activity, after the work is done. This may be found in the sense of accomplishment, the opportunity to look at our handiwork, the ability to reflect on our place, our role in the beauty, the growth, even the cycle of life.

In the company of plants one is a companion to life, shares a place in the universe. When we are doing the rewarding work of gardening, even in the drudgery of it, we are positively focused. It's after the work is done that we can step back, relax and truly enjoy what has been accomplished. We have worked together with God, by what ever name you choose to call this universal force, to create beauty. We unleash our senses to absorb all the impressions, sensations and experiences of discovery. After the work is done, we can bathe in the wonder of it all; we can refresh the soul. We can know harmony and peace.

It's common for those troubled to seek the quiet garden as a place to meditate, to think, to pray, to restore energy. In England a movement called Quiet Gardens was started a few years ago. It has spread to a number of countries and provides a blend of Christianity with the comfort of the garden. In the Muslim world numerous gardens exist as oases in the spiritual desert. The Buddhists find peace and oneness in the garden. Most of the sacred places of the world are gardens, either natural or crafted by human need for beauty.

In the delicate petals of the tiniest flower
I see the face of God.
In the breeze that makes the grass dance
I feel his life-giving breath.
In the callused bark of the ancient oak
I am protected by his strength.
In the promise of the dry dust-like seed
I am comforted by his gift of life.
Anon

Some go to the garden to meditate, not because there is nothing happening there, but because of the intensity of its reality. Many are even called to write within the inspirational serenity of the garden. So much of the human soul is defined in the poetry that flows from us when we are in the community of plants. In this community we are not only closer to nature, we are in the midst of it, in fact we are a part of it.

This passive appreciation of the garden and the meditation that can be experienced there doesn't have to wait until the work is done. In fact, spending some time in quiet contemplation of the potential of what can be achieved in the garden is often more valuable than reflecting on what has been done.

One of my fondest childhood memories involved the arrival of the seeds catalogs in the mail. The timing was perfect because Christmas was over, and the cold white face of winter was staring in the window. Mom would make hot chocolate and, with a plate of left over Christmas cookies, that evening the family gathered around the kitchen table and planted in our minds next spring's garden. We would compare the virtues of each variety of beans, squash and tomato, note the must try novelty plants, and talk of the fruit trees we wanted to add to the orchard. Dad would look out the window of the old farmhouse and see the rows of sweetcorn, smell the tomato vines, and picture the baskets of carrots and beets in his mind. He planted his garden on those snowy January evenings. Mom planned the flowers that would grace the rock garden, what she wanted to grow to take to the cemetery on Memorial Day, which annuals were to go around the back porch this year. She too could visualize the herb garden, the bed of glads and the strawberries that were always her pride and joy. This was horticultural therapy most valued because it gave hope in the depths of depression inducing winter. We, as a family made spring into an anticipated promise of vitality and joy.

By mentally and emotionally preparing ourselves we are creating a vision, a goal, a purpose. Then we commence the journey, a journey of personal discovery.

Dr. Diane Relf, Professor of Horticulture, makes this statement in *Dynamics of Horticultural Therapy* Rehab. Lit. 42:147-150, 1981.

From being around plants, from observing their growth, man acquires an understanding of life and the rhythms that maintain it. From plants man derives a sense of "dynamic stability through change," Without continuous change, plants could not survive. A plant must flower in order to set seed; it must go dormant to survive the winter. There is a natural rhythm, a time and a season for all things, and nothing can be forced out of its natural order and still survive.

The Spiritual Connection Between Plants and People

For those who can move beyond the concept of the garden as a place of work into an understanding of the peace and beauty to be found and nourished there, great comfort and happiness are the reward. This is a spiritual journey for which many aren't yet ready. Many others need help to find their own path; many others are standing at the open gate. There is an undeniable restorative power in active or passive participation with the natural world. There are a number of theories on why this is so.

- For some it's the challenge, either of their mastery of self or artistry. For there is great art in the garden, and it is art of the moment.
- It's a matter of evolution. We are instinctively drawn to the wilderness home with its open expanse, its freedom.
- Being away from all the tension, pressure, interruption and artificial structure of modern living.
- Sense of intrigue and adventure. There is always mystery in the garden, always something new to discover and savor. When we connect with the great mystery of existence, this is perhaps the greatest adventure of all.
- Perceptual stimulation and total exercise of the senses is another aspect of the gardening experience. Even our senses beyond the physical are exercised as we know the life of the garden.
- We find acceptance and compatibility in the natural setting of the garden. In essence we become unified with the life around us, we become a part of something much greater than we are.
- We are forced to focus on other. Our problems and pains are forced into the background as we unite with our living environment. We concentrate on what is around us and in that way discover ourselves.
- The garden, even if it is confined to the windowsill or patio, broadens our vision, expands our horizon, encourages us to see beyond yesterday into the promise of tomorrow.
- We find wisdom and beauty growing there. These are spiritual treasures that enrich the soul.

We often think of the garden as nature tamed by the hand of man, but, perhaps it's more appropriate to think of it as humanity embraced by the inviting arms of nature. Sometimes opening the soul to beauty is activity enough. Connecting with another living entity can, if we will permit it, be an inspirational experience. To feel the leaves, to smell the flowers, to be a part of the cycle of life and growth is to give the gift of hope and a reason for tomorrow. Sometimes *being* is activity enough.

A Garden Is the Library of Life

Instinctively grasping the restorative value of the garden as a place to visit, royalty has for thousands of years expended great sums on the creation of calm beauty. From the hanging gardens of Babylon to the court of Versailles, the garden was valued more than gold. When a Chinese empress was faced with the decision of rebuilding the navy or the royal gardens, she chose the gardens. There all the people could benefit every day. In the United States the wealthy established a wonderful legacy with the gardens on their estates. The DuPonts at Longwood Gardens in Pennsylvania and the Leus and Fairchilds in Florida are only a few examples.

In ancient Egypt, mental patients were taken for strolls through the pharaohs' gardens. European monks built monastic gardens for meditation, as did their counterparts in Tibet. Great gardens were created as a tribute to great love. This all speaks to humanity's need for connection with the beauty of life. The ancient civilizations accepted this as a natural part of their existence. Somewhere along the way, through the winding river of years, some of us came to disparage anything that didn't have practical value. A garden that didn't put food on the table was a waste of time. Every plant had to have a purpose or it was a weed. We came to view nature as the enemy and brazenly took up arms against the Mother Earth herself. We lost sight of the therapeutic value for the spirit that can be found in the garden.

There is much to be said for simply being with plants. Sitting in the room where they live, sharing their sun along a garden path or experiencing the comforting shade of a sheltering tree. In these simple places, we connect with our instinctive needs and visit our God.

We don't have to always be working. In our contemporary culture, we even work at playing. We can't get off the treadmill, we can't escape the phone, we can't take a few minutes to find ourselves. We have lost our rhythm, our balance. Passively sitting or walking through a garden isn't a waste of time or a sin. Quite the contrary, it's time well spent in prayer. It permits us discovery of the sense of peace we have within us, just waiting for the opportunity to grow.

PART THREE
PUTTING IT ALL TOGETHER

Chapter 12
Special Gardens for Special Populations

Stan was twenty when the police brought him to the group home for the mentally retarded. He could only speak a few words, ate with his hands and lacked the coordination to get around the room without stumbling and tripping. After several weeks, one of the nurses who had been caring for him made a discovery that changed his life. He wasn't retarded, he was blind.

Stan's parents were so ashamed of him as a child that he never went to school, never got to play with any other children, but his father would take him out for a walk almost every evening after dark. He was walked on a leash, like a dog.

In a matter of months he was learning language skills, social skills and being fitted with special glasses that would make limited vision possible. Even after all this, he lived in the fog shrouded world of the legally blind. Then he received an invitation to take part in a new program that was providing training in horticultural skills for the disabled. While this was designed as horticultural therapy, the ultimate objective was to train the students for careers.

Within a month Stan was the star student in his "garden school." He would sit bent over at the bench planting seeds and cuttings mostly by feel. He graduated to the hanging baskets, learned how to feed, water and trim. By the end of the third month he was teaching the others. Because his childhood had been so barren of intellectual stimulation he couldn't become fully independent, but the progress he made was awesome. His ability to communicate was the most restricted, but he thoroughly enjoyed working with the herb hanging baskets, and could identify all of the plants he grew by feel or fragrance.

A Brief History of Horticultural Therapy in America

Horticultural therapy programs for the mentally disabled have been around for a long time. In fact, the first HT program in this country was started in Philadelphia by Dr. Benjamin Rush, one of the signers of the Declaration of Independence and considered by many to be the father of psychiatry, in 1798. From observation he concluded that labor in a farm setting had a positive and curative effect on the mentally ill. His was a concept of active, engaged involvement by the patient.

The Friends Hospital, in Pennsylvania, created the first private psychiatric institution in America in 1817. This "Asylum for Persons Deprived of Their Reason" took a more passive approach by creating shaded walks, winding forest paths and open expanses of rolling field and meadow.

Today many psychologists and psychiatrists treat their patients by strolling through a non-threatening environment with them. The safe and quiet garden is a part of the recovery program in many rehabilitation programs.

In the late 1800's New York City was a hotbed of horticultural therapy activity. The Children's Aid Society was one of the first to use gardening as a way to help the disadvantaged young people living in the tenements. Today we call them inner city youth, but their needs haven't changed.

At the same time the "Flower Missions" were collecting flowers and delivering bouquets to hospitals, homes of the aged and asylums for the infirm. Many garden clubs today carry on this tradition. Wouldn't it be great if florist shops and garden centers promoted such a program and donated some of their less salable wares to these institutions.

C. F. Menninger and his son, Karl, created the Menninger Foundation in Topeka, Kansas in 1919. Gardening and nature study were an integral part of the treatment program for their patients. This has been replicated in many similar institutions throughout the world, and the trend is gaining momentum as we seek respite from the pressures of the technological society we've created.

During World War II, the concept of horticultural therapy was brought to new heights by the garden clubs throughout the world. They gave tirelessly of their time, expertise and gardens to bring flowers and the experience of gardening to thousands of soldiers and civilians who needed therapy and rehabilitation. Today, for many garden clubs this sharing of themselves continues to be one of their major activities.

The gradual development of this concept of the gardening experience as a form of therapy has culminated in a professional classification, horticultural therapy, complete with college training programs and a professional organization. It was through the Menninger Foundation that the first horticultural therapy training program was established at Kansas State University. The American Horticultural Therapy Association and its state chapters are working hard to bring the benefits of gardening as therapy to a multitude of special populations.

Gardening with Limitations

All of us function with limitations. There is a strong temptation to look down from some lofty seat of superiority and make judgments about those who are different. Too many of us look the other way and pretend the disabled don't exist. It's so easy to blame them for their own misfortune, but the simple fact is that we share all of these limitations in mind, body and spirit. The difference is only a matter of degree. We share their limitations, and they share ours. That's what living in a community requires. Horticultural therapy is one of the ways we can share our burdens.

We call them special populations: the blind, those with hearing impairment, the multitude of us who are confined to wheelchairs, those of us who have lost limbs, or the use of them, stroke patients, those of us who contend daily with chronic disease, the abused and the abusers, children who have lost their way in school, our neighbors who are mentally disabled, struggling to recover from addiction, loneliness, depression or mental illness. These are a few of the special populations that horticultural therapists work with daily. It takes special training to bring someone back from profound depression, to guide a paraplegic in the art of living through gardening, help a stroke patient regain the confidence to try, or give a developmentally disabled person pleasant experiences, valuable skills and perhaps a career.

Horticultural therapists can be found in a multitude of health care facilities and social service organizations. They are a part of a team of health care professionals and social workers. They can also be found in the workplace where they help prevent burnout, or in senior communities where they make gardening the link between yesterday and tomorrow. They serve as consultants, train volunteer staffs and establish programs. Horticultural therapists are a part of a team that helps to make life livable and hope possible for millions.

Who Uses Horticultural Therapy?

Nursing homes

Alzheimer's care facilities

Senior day care centers

Hospice agencies and programs

Grief recovery programs

Assisted living communities

Cancer treatment facilities

Hospitals

Rehabilitation units

Community mental health agencies

Shelters for abuse victims

Homeless shelters

Correctional institutions

Facilities for the developmentally
    disabled

Mental health facilities

Veterans Administration

Community parks & rec.

Public housing agencies

Agencies for the blind

Group homes

Vocational training programs

Substance abuse programs

Children's advocacy groups

School systems

Programs for at-risk youth

Early intervention programs

Environmental programs

Multi-generational programs

Enlightened businesses

The Children

Not very many years ago, most children grew up in a rural setting. The family farm was home, and working in the family garden was what children did. This labor spent with parents and siblings gave them a sense of purpose, a sense of belonging, a connection to not only the soil, but also to the family. This agricultural experience was satisfying to the instincts we all possess to work together, to nurture and harvest. These are our true survival instincts.

In the city were the tenements, the bricks, where the newest wave of immigrants found shelter while discovering a new way of life. Even there one could find flowers, potted plants and window boxes that were a link to the green world. Today the inner city is often a desert devoid of the garden, possessing only islands of green in the form of municipal parks. The children lose the family connection and the people-plant connection. We have generations that can't communicate with each other because they lack the communion of shared activity.

In the sixties and seventies we saw the beginning of a wave of community gardens, block gardens, roof gardens and beautification programs. We saw urban greening, an explosion of parks construction and a renewed sense of community. This trend continues today as schools have gardens, vacant lots become places of pride where cross-generational understanding is nurtured, the global garden becomes a multi-cultural experience, and real people become accepted as role models.

The term at-risk youth is used to denote those of our children who may fall into the cycle of alcohol, drugs, violence or crime. In truth, all children are "at-risk youths." As a community, we all have an obligation to prepare our children to be active in body, alert in mind, and strong in spirit.

Horticultural activity, of course, isn't the answer for everyone, but it is an acceptable way for our children to learn to work together toward a common goal, experience success, be a positive force in their community. Growing plants on the school grounds, planting and maintaining a school landscape, or adopting a section of a community park gives our children a chance to hear positive words rather than "don't do that," and "you can't."

Teens with addictions, children who have been abused, children who have been taught that violence is the answer, youths in juvenile facilities and prisons should have the opportunity to heal and grow. Horticultural therapy programs can help. We don't have to be a nation that, like ferrets, eats its young. Our children don't have to be hopeless.

After consulting with a horticultural therapist that worked out of a local botanical garden, an elementary school group turned a section of their school grounds into a vegetable garden. The produce went to a local food bank and homeless shelter. These kids were not only proud of the garden they grew, they were proud of their positive role in the community. At another school, a group of troubled teens grew plants and flowers and gave them to the residents of a local nursing home.

What greater gift can we give our children than the opportunity to care and share? Children have such energy and drive, are so eager to learn, and need so much to be a part of something, to belong. We can, as a community, use horticultural therapists to create programs that cross generational and cultural barriers, give a positive outlet to the stress of being youth rather than drugs, show that there are other options than violence, other peer groups than gangs.

This isn't just the role of schools, this is an obligation of the entire community. Municipal departments of parks and recreation can tap into this valuable volunteer resource. The scouts, church groups and the 4-H can be community activists, clearing, planting, growing, serving. Civic and professional organizations can promote, fund, sponsor and participate in the positive expression of youth. Businesses can also promote and sponsor programs that grow a sense of responsibility. This is a cheap investment in tomorrow, but it's a good one.

Developmental Disabilities

It is a simple fact that many infants enter the world with physical and mental limitations. This can range from mild to profound. A developmental disability can originate before birth or in childhood. It isn't something that will go away, but it is a condition that we as individuals and as a society must deal with. Many of these people will never be able to be self sufficient, never be able to hold a job, raise a family, even dress themselves or tie their own shoes. Others will be able to learn skills that can permit them a role in society, even if it's limited to a shelter workshop. Every individual is entitled to dignity, respect as a fellow human being, and quality of life. Developmental disabilities include Downe's syndrome, autism, spinal bifida, cerebral palsy, fetal alcohol syndrome and cocaine babies, to list only a few.

One of the greatest challenges for the horticultural therapist is to develop special tools to aid those with a limited ability to function or perform some of the basic gardening tasks. Some of these people may not be able to use limbs, but creative horticultural therapists have developed tools that strap onto the head, or are held in the mouth.

John Matthes, past president of the Florida Chapter of the American Horticultural Therapy Association gave me a demonstration of several of these tools and techniques. They range from guides to use when taking cuttings, to movable frames that make it easy to set pots in rows. Some of these are solutions to problems that most of us don't encounter.

In a workshop where the students are filling pots with soil in preparation for seeding or striking cuttings, one of the difficulties often encountered is their ability to get the right amount of soil in the pot. Sometimes it will be heaped in an overflowing mound, other times the pot will be less than half full. What John does is teach them to overfill the pot, then level it off by running a piece of dowel over across the rim. To prevent gouging into the soil, a plastic bottle cap can be stapled to each end of the dowel.

Benefits

For the developmentally disabled, horticultural therapy holds tremendous potential benefits.

Psychological By participating in a gardening activity the natural, instinctive link between people and plants is established. This provides a level of comfort and sense of place and belonging. By experiencing success with plants, and by mastering the skills required, the individual also grows his or her sense of self-worth, self-esteem and self-confidence. There is also the opportunity to find self-expression, engage in creative exercises and experience the discovery of links between action and result. A satisfying sense of accomplishment is one of the benefits we all grow in the garden.

Physical Gardening provides an exercise program that can be tailor made for the individual. It encourages the reaching, stretching and bending that improve muscle tone, coordination and circulation. For some this exercise may be in the form of raking leaves, spreading mulch, weeding and watering. For others, the activities may be limited to a workbench. Physical skills are developed. Exposure to fresh air and sunshine is both physically and mentally advantageous to all of us.

Mental ability Cognitive skills are exercised and nurtured in the gardening experience, as well as the physical. The ability to reason is encouraged and stimulated in the communion with plants. As verbal skills are used, proficiency increases. Vocabulary increases as the desire to communicate grows. The concepts of quantity, numbers and math develop with the physical contact with seeds, pots, trays, etc. We all learn in the garden. It may be as simple as seasons, where we learn to accept our internal rhythm as we come to understand the cycle. We learn about other climates and cultures, beauty and botany, but most of all we learn about life.

Social skills Many people with developmental disabilities haven't found the skills necessary for social interaction. Horticultural therapy programs provide an opportunity for group effort, shared experiences, and the confidence to interact that comes from possessing an ability or talent. The physical activity of gardening provides an outlet for frustration and aggression. It's socially acceptable to vent anger on the weeds. Field trips to parks and gardens can be a social experience as well as a learning opportunity.

The possession of skills opens the door to sharing with the community. Programs for the developmentally disabled can bring these people into the community through plant sales, participation in garden shows, fairs, special events and community programs. They can share the produce of their gardens with local food banks, and the flowers they grow with nursing homes, schools and community centers. We can all share our gardening experiences. These people may have physical and mental limitations, but there is no limit to their joy and enthusiasm, if only we will take a few minutes to share and learn from each other. Communicating with other gardeners is fun.

Careers The developmentally disabled have a difficult time finding their role in the workplace. The horticulture industry has a multitude of jobs that match the skill levels of many of these individuals. It becomes the horticultural therapist's role to not only develop the basic skills required in working with plants, but the soft skills of the workplace as well. These include dependability, staying on task, accepting assignment, accepting criticism and correction, getting to work on time, dressing appropriately, following direction and working with others. In the process, concepts like integrity and responsibility also need to be acquired. The advantage is that these are skills that can accompany these individuals into a fuller, richer life and even into other career fields. Vocational therapy can be a vital part of a comprehensive horticultural therapy program.

Mental Illness

Mental illness is usually divided into four categories.
- **Mood disorders** include depression, which can inhibit one's ability to feel pleasure, influence appetite, sleep patterns, impedes concentration and energy levels. Bipolar disorder is the alternation between depression and a feeling of euphoria called mania that can include sleeplessness, delusions of grandeur, a sense of omnipotence, hyperactivity and impulsive behavior.
- **Anxiety** disorders can include frequent and severe fears, phobias or panic-attacks, obsessive-compulsive behavior or post-traumatic stress syndrome. Depending on severity,

anxiety disorders can seriously interfere with an individual's ability to function in the family, workplace or society.

- **Cognitive** disorders involve the ability of the mind to receive information, process, store and react to it. This can involve memory, speech, sense of time and place, ability to communicate with others and make needs known. This can be a result of stroke, medication, drugs, brain injury or diseases such as Alzheimer's.
- **Psychotic** disorders involve a loss of connection with reality. This can be in the form of hallucination, body sensations, or paranoia. Schizophrenia and other psychotic disorders can limit the ability to care for oneself or be a part of society.

A horticultural therapist working with the mentally ill is a part of a treatment team. The therapeutic value of gardening for the mentally ill is basically the same as it is for all of us. The patient is in a non-threatening, non-demanding environment where he or she can exercise some measure of control. The opportunity to nurture, to be a part of the growth process makes the journey the objective. The horticultural experience empowers by giving the patient new knowledge, or the refreshing connection with forgotten experiences. With the new skills comes new confidence.

With all this is the instinctive comfort we feel in the garden. It has been argued that much of the stress we experience today is because we have literally imprisoned ourselves in sterile cages with artificial sound, light and air. We exist devoid of life; our need for adventure and discovery remains unfulfilled. These are the psychological needs we instinctively possess, and for our minds and bodies to function properly we need to exercise these needs. Mastering the skills to face and survive these aspects of life give us the ability to make rational judgments, know joy and be a participant in our own reality rather than a virtual existence. We also encourage gardening activity with the mentally ill as a way to lead them to a sense of self worth and the confidence to engage in social activity. In programs developed by horticultural therapists aggression can be decreased, channeled or controlled, patients can learn how to assume responsibility, overcome feelings of inadequacy, develop their sense of beauty, learn nurturing skills, and acquire social skills. The therapeutic program may begin with passive experiencing of the garden or nature trail. This may be followed by combined passive-active involvement in a gardening program. As the patient progresses, creative projects and group activities can be used as non-threatening avenues back to a place in the community. It should be noted that horticultural therapy isn't the only treatment tool, but it can be valuable when used with medications and psychiatric treatment.

Limited Mobility

Thousands of people each year become mobility impaired through strokes, disease, surgery or accident. For some this is temporary and through time and therapy, most functioning is regained. A stroke patient may have to learn to walk again, how to use his or her hand and arm. Surgery on bones or muscles will require the services of a physical therapist as recovery progresses.

Many others face a lifetime in a wheelchair, or a future without an arm or leg. This is a devastating blow, but fortunately there are people and programs to help these individuals adjust, cope and assume an active life again. Professional horticultural therapists on the staffs of rehabilitation centers, treatment facilities and botanical gardens work closely with the rest of the health care team to create therapy programs. The objective is to improve the attitude of the patient as his or her latitude of activity is increased.

There is tremendous value to the mind, body and soul in passively experiencing the garden. To be surrounded by life that is growing, blooming, fragrant, colorful, in so many ways dynamic is healing. To sit by the fountain and watch the play of sun and shadow, hear the splash of the water and witness the dance of the leaves can be a therapeutic experience. However, to accomplish this, the garden must be accessible.

Active participation in the gardening experience requires more than wider paths. To open the door of opportunity for the mobility impaired to do gardening requires special garden design, tools and growing techniques. Gene Rothert, in his wonderful book *The Enabling Garden: Creating Barrier-Free Gardens* discusses a multitude of ways that accessibility to both the garden and gardening can be achieved.

The opportunity to work in the comfortable and accepting arena of the garden can have a positive influence on the attitude because there the patients are able to nurture, and see positive results from their efforts. The ability to be a positive force in their environment is as emotionally uplifting as it is physically beneficial.

Adapting the Garden: Whether the limitations are temporary or permanent these will be some adaptations needed to bring the garden and the gardener together.

- The more level the site, the easier the use will be.
- Access ramps and railings
- Clear wide paths. The average wheelchair is 30" wide. A well planned path will permit two wheelchairs to pass.
- Paths with very coarse, soft or sandy textures are difficult for wheelchair traffic.
- Edgings to mark paths can be helpful for those with vision impairment.
- Container gardening elevates the plants to a level that permits ease of activity for the gardener, while retaining aesthetic appeal.
- Raised beds also provide accessibility for those who are confined to a wheelchair, or have trouble stooping or kneeling.

- Hanging baskets can be on pulleys for easy access from a wheelchair.
- Work stations and potting benches are available that permit easy use from a wheelchair.
- Wall gardens, the uses of trellises, arbors and pergolas puts the plants within reach.
- Growing dwarf trees permits easy harvest from a wheelchair.

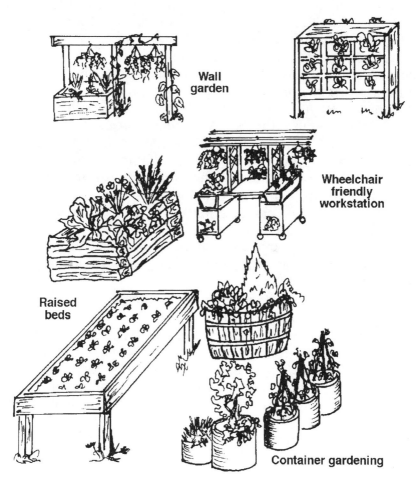

Adaptive growing techniques

Adapting the tools: To understand how difficult it is to garden with limitations, try roaming your yard in a wheelchair, or tape your fingers together so that gripping ability is similar to that of someone with arthritis. Try to garden with one hand tied behind your back. Many tool manufacturers are now producing hand tools that are user friendly for those with limited mobility. These ergonomically designed tools also make gardening easier for all of us. Special shears, trowels with comfort grips, tools with extended handles, long handled tools with extra grips are a part of the manufactured arsenal.

Horticultural therapists are a resourceful and creative lot and a multitude of adaptations to standard tools have come into use. A section of foam insulation pipe wrap can turn an inexpensive hand trowel or cultivator into something usable by someone with arthritis. A standard hand trowel fastened to the end of a piece of PVC pipe extends the reach and helps to make ground level beds workable. A piece of PVC pipe with a slanted cut on one end makes a great seeding tool that permits planting without bending, stooping or kneeling. The hole can be created, the seed dropped into the pipe, then covered, all in one smooth motion.

The following are some of the tool considerations and adaptations that can make gardening possible for those with mobility limitations.

- Lightweight tools are easier to handle.
- Labeling, colorful flags to mark work areas.
- Brightly colored handles to prevent loss.
- Gloves with Velcro strips that match strips on the tools.
- Straps on hands, wrists and arms that can hold tools.
- A mirror glued on a golf club (putter) permits easy viewing under the leaves to search for fruit or insect pests.
- Attachable extension handles to increase reach from wheelchair.

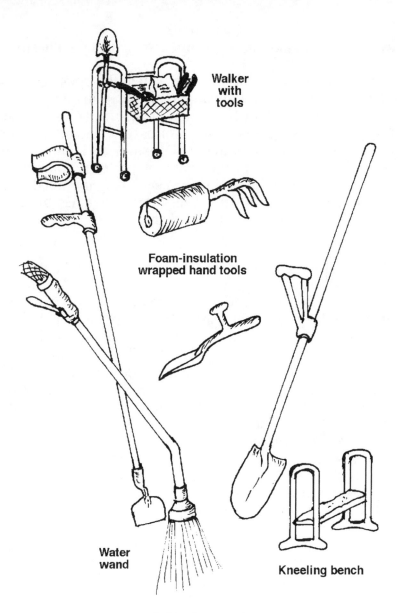

Walker with tools

Foam-insulation wrapped hand tools

Water wand

Kneeling bench

Adaptive tools

95

Chapter 13
The Socially Disadvantaged and Horticultural Therapy

There are many people who are denied the opportunity to enter the mainstream of contemporary life. This may be the result of poverty, lack of education, mental instability, abuse, drugs, and this list could continue for pages. The urban poor, those residing in subsidized housing and immigrant neighborhoods don't feel the sense of pride in community that can be found in the suburbs. Yet in neighborhood after neighborhood, these residents are joining together to clean up and reclaim, beautify and take charge.

A Community That Gardens Together Grows Together

Vacant lots can become community gardens where produce can be grown and shared. People on limited incomes can stretch their food budget, exercise body and mind, eat healthier, and learn to work together. The blending of the generations and cultures that occur within the confines of a community garden can, and do, promote acceptance, understanding and cooperation. Both adults and children are taking charge of their life and their destiny.

The greening of the inner-city answers that instinctive need for sense of place, security and comfort that dwells within us all, regardless of our income or where we live. The garden experience provides an alternative to drugs, violence, hopelessness, depression and aggression. The garden may be found on the rooftop, or in a windowbox, or it might be remote from the residence. Regardless of where it is, the entire community benefits. When hope is restored to an individual, wonderful things can happen. The same is true for a neighborhood. Drugs can be replaced with fertilizer, gardening can replace violence, beauty can replace decay, and a vision of a better tomorrow can replace pessimism.

It doesn't matter if the initiative comes from the community leaders, horticultural therapists or residents. The beauty is that when these three work together, miracles can happen. For more information on creating community gardens see page 119.

Without a Home

The people we today call homeless are rarely there by choice. Many are the mentally ill that society is no longer willing to care for in an institutional setting. Some are on the streets because of a lack of training or illiteracy. Some have followed a bottle or drugs to the street. Others have been unable to weather crises in career, family or relationship. Some have lost their way spiritually, while others are suffering physical limitations. There isn't a single cause for homelessness, nor is there a single cure.

Horticultural therapists can help some of these people regain a sense of place and pride when they use gardening as therapy. This may be in the form of a garden at a homeless shelter, spending time in a community garden, or working to help establish and maintain a garden for other special populations. The opportunity to produce some of the food consumed in the shelter, and the opportunity to contribute to the community is spiritually uplifting. It also opens the door to alternatives, options and possibilities.

Homelessness isn't a problem that can be eliminated by some generous act from individuals or groups who assume a sense of benevolent superiority. Homelessness requires the combined efforts of an understanding and empathetic community. This isn't a problem that can be removed from sight with vagrancy laws, prison time, or a handout. Blaming the victim isn't the answer to this problem. In fact, this is a problem that doesn't need to exist. This is a side of our culture we all need to know more about. When churches, local government, civic organizations, health care professions and horticultural therapists join forces to provide treatment, counseling, education, life skills and motivation, we can open the door to a life complete with a sense of dignity and purpose.

Horticultural therapy programs can provide a safe, non-judgmental place, a connection, or re-connection, with life, and a reason for tomorrow. At the same time, productive skills are explored and learned, social skills developed, and spiritual growth experienced. The garden is, after all, a restorative environment.

Prison Gardens

Inmates growing their own food is nothing new. As a part of rehabilitation programs, there can be tremendous value in horticulture, both as therapy and as vocational training. Many of the offenders serving time come from low-income, inner-city, high unemployment environments. There isn't incentive to pursue education and establish positive career goals, follow the example of positive role models, or spend time in personal reflection. This simply isn't a part of that culture.

A horticultural training program for prisons will include an opportunity for cooperative effort, learning experiences, the creation of beauty, the connection with life itself, and the spiritual side of the green experience. For people who may have never worked in a garden, there are valuable lessons to be learned.

- The value of planning ahead, of setting goals.
- Experiencing delayed gratification, and the value of positive expectation.
- How to adapt to changing conditions.
- Communicating and working cooperatively.
- Negative consequences of neglect.
- Pride in success.
- Self-esteem that can come from a productive work experience.
- Reflection and self discovery.
- Time for the inmate to think about a future. Metaphorically he or she can grow as well as the plants being cultivated.

Inmate comments on horticultural therapy programs include the following. "To grow something taught me to appreciate life more than I thought possible." "You taught me a lot more than horticulture. You taught me self-respect, self-worth, and dignity." "Thank you for treating me as a person."

Many of the best programs in prisons and correctional institutions are inmate initiated, then actively pursued by the correctional staff that is more concerned with rehabilitation than punishment. Perhaps it is possible to grow at least some of the incarcerated out of the life style that led them to crime. This will never be a 100% solution, but neither is the perpetual imprisonment of so many of our fellow human beings. If we can't provide a better example than one of vengeance, anger, violence and retribution, then haven't we proven to the inmate that the attitudes that landed him or her in prison are socially valid; the only difference between them and us is that they got caught? If we react in kind to the anti-social actions they took, what lessons are we learning ourselves?

Drugs and Alcohol

Drugs and alcohol are, for many, a means of escape, a way to flee a situation that can't be controlled, handled, dealt with or tolerated. For others, it's a way to escape from themselves, their limitations, their past, their perceived lack of future, their sense of failure. When we can no longer cope without these supports, then we are under their control, and we have become our own worst victim.

Unfortunately, when an individual is being held prisoner by substance abuse, others suffer too. The family and community lose a productive member. Morality, and the sense of right and wrong are lost in the shrouds of addiction. Violence becomes a means of coping, of sating the demon's desire. The addict's self-image is too weakened to permit him or her to alter the course without intervention. The work of substance abuse programs begins with a reclaiming of self. Much of the best horticultural therapy work today is being done in the setting of such treatment centers. Again, there is a calm, non-threatening environment where the individual can progress at his or her own pace. The recovering individual has time for reflection, and positive self-motivation. Small victories are celebrated and shared as hope is restored. The horticultural therapist is only one member of a team that helps to retrain mind, body and soul.

Isn't it unfortunate that most of this reclamation of humanity is only available to those with sufficient resources? The poor, the mentally and emotionally disturbed, the hopeless from the inner-city looking for a way out, desperately seeking any escape, are condemned to suffer as outcasts, when they could be transformed into active, productive individuals.

Because abuse affects everyone of us socially and economically, we need to re-examine our attitudes toward the problem. Would programs that remove the hopelessness and barrenness of life help these people? Is it worth the effort to combine the many facets of the community to reduce the demand for drugs, not by imprisoning the substance abusers, but by truly setting them free? Could the solution start to grow in the security and comfort of a garden?

Abuse Victims and the Abusers

For a certain segment of our society, violence is the answer to a multitude of questions, and the response to many situations. This pattern is often inherited from the past generation, but it's a cycle that can be broken. Unfortunately, most of the victims are emotionally scared long after the wounds are healed. Many women and children become convinced that they deserved the abuse, and enter into a cycle themselves.

In shelters, group homes and programs for victims of sexual abuse and violence, one of the first objectives is to create a sense of safety and security. Then efforts are made to gain a sense of self-worth and self-esteem. Horticultural therapists have put together successful programs that involve a safe and comfortable garden setting, often beginning as a passive experience. Connection with life is re-established. As these individuals begin to assume an active role in the garden, they begin to take command of their own lives as well. A garden can be an empowering, liberating, comforting and rewarding place. It can provide the reason to get out of bed, think ahead, and visualize a positive future.

On the practical side, for the abuse victims without job skills, the horticultural therapy program can open doors to a self sufficient career, or a home garden that can help with the food bill.

For children caught in the cycle of abuse, the garden can become a place where that cycle of violence and anger is replaced with other cycles of the seasons, planting and harvest, anticipation and realization of beauty. They can learn more acceptable methods of expressing anger, disappointment and frustration. The program that teaches them they can have a hand in their destiny, that they can change, is a program that can free them and their children from this cycle of violence. When individuals can enjoy a sense of place, a sense of belonging, a sense of beauty and a sense of safety, they have the power to set themselves free from their past.

When someone is set on the path of abusiveness, it's because they feel that their life is out of their control. They respond in the only way they know how. Sometimes this is fueled by alcohol or drugs. Sometimes it is fed by insecurity and low self-image. Control of someone else becomes the focus, when we feel that we cannot control ourselves. Not all abusers of spouses and children can be helped by horticultural training programs, but some can be. It requires a team of counseling professionals, but learning the same patience skills that were discussed with inmates can help.

Daylily

Chapter 14
Senior Populations

The elderly are the fastest growing population in America and most of the rest of the world. There are a multitude of reasons why senior citizens should engage in gardening. Some of these reasons are physically or mentally therapeutic. Often the distinction is drawn between horticultural therapy and therapeutic horticulture. For purposes of this book, we will leave that debate to the purists who have time. All gardening can be therapeutic. Look at what a senior citizen can gain from the experience.

- Gardening is great exercise, and it can be self-paced.
- There is the satisfaction factor of taking something from seed to fruit, or cutting to flower.
- The gardener is needed by the plants. This is a comfortable blend of need and responsibility.
- Gardening gives the senior citizen a future to look forward to, literally demanding a faith in the future.
- Gardening can be a shared experience, a focal point for conversation, companionship and group activity.
- Gardening is fun. It makes people smile.

Many retirement communities have garden clubs, as do a growing number of assisted living facilities. Senior community centers and senior daycare programs frequently use horticulture as one of their activities. One of the advantages here is that gardening isn't gender specific, both men and women can, and do, enjoy the activity. Nursing homes, Alzheimer's care units and hospice facilities are also using horticultural therapy programs.

Dr. J. Thomas, M.D. developed the Eden Alternative program after working as a geriatric specialist. He likened the average nursing home to a desert where three things dominated: loneliness, boredom and depression. It was his idea that plants, pets and children should be a part of the nursing home's daily experience. Horticultural therapy programs have carried this a step beyond the passive living with plants, to actively cultivating them. Again, this isn't the answer for every elderly individual, but for those who have entered into such programs, medication needs have decreased and physical complaints have been reduced. The exercise and social exchange, the acquiring and utilizing of new knowledge and skills even reduces confusion in many seniors. Regular horticultural therapy sessions increase social interaction as well.

The elderly carry their badges of survival and its scars. Most older people have chronic conditions to cope with. About half of all senior citizens know intimately the pain and discomfort of arthritis. At least a third of our seniors have high blood pressure, hypertension. Heart disease, strokes and circulation problems afflict another third of the aged population. Most senior citizens have hearing impairment, and many experience tintinitus and difficulty with balance. Most seniors also have some vision loss, including cataracts, ability to distinguish color, distance, adjust to light changes and loss of peripheral vision. Diabetes carries with it a number of other health problems. Horticultural therapy programs won't reverse these conditions, but they can provide exercises that can slow the progress of some, and the means to cope with others. It's a matter of giving purpose, meaning and worth to someone's existence.

When my mother was in her last months of life, the congestive heart failure was progressively denying her more and more of her ability to function. Until the last two weeks, she continued to strike cuttings of ivy and begonias, creating gifts for the "nice folks at hospice." From her wheelchair, then bedside, she continued to watch over her African violets and other house plants. She smiled a lot when she talked about her plants. Horticultural therapy put meaning in her final months, gave her the dignity of joy.

Alzheimer's Patients

Alzheimer's disease is the most common form of dementia in our senior population. It's a chronic, degenerative and irreversible condition that affects the part of the brain that controls thought, memory and language. It's estimated that over fourteen million Americans will be suffering from Alzheimer's disease as this new millennium begins. Onset and progression is gradual. Memory loss, disorientation, impaired judgment and abstract reasoning, periods of confusion, wandering, anxiety, withdrawal and aggression are some of the manifestations of this disease that occur when the brain cells die. Current research is making some great strides, but as yet there are no cures. Fortunately, it isn't a normal part of aging.

Horticultural therapists can put together effective programs that can provide the following to Alzheimer's victims.

- Improvement and maintenance of physical health through activities.
- Encourage self-care independence.
- Maintain or improve social interaction.
- Exercise the memory and reasoning.
- Create a positive quality of life through meaningful activity.
- People with Alzheimer's disease can find comfort in the routine of gardening.
- Both passive and active gardening experiences can be beneficial and enjoyable to the Alzheimer's patient.
- Family members can share in the horticultural experience.

Often overlooked are the needs of the family caregiver of an Alzheimer's patient. Theirs is a never-ending vigil with an overwhelming amount of stress.

Horticultural Therapy
for Those with Dementia and Alzheimer's Disease

When a horticultural therapist designs a program for patients with these progressive diseases there are several factors that must be considered.

- **Personal memories** can be triggered by the colors, scents and textures of the garden. These memories of past activities and pleasures can help bring comfort and understanding to the patient.

- **A walled enclosure** is a good idea for the safety of the patient who may wander with no knowledge of how to return.

- **A water feature** is of tremendous value. This may be in the form of a small stream, a fountain, or a pool where hands can be dipped. The sound and feel of water is soothing, refreshing and stimulating to the senses.

- **A canopy** of trees, arbors or trellises can provide shade and a sense of security, but it should be open enough to permit an expansive view.

- **Well defined paths** are necessary to help provide direction to patient wandering. It's best if the paths are winding, rather than straight. This provides a stimulating sense of adventure.

- **Benches,** picnic tables and well defined resting areas are also important.

- **Vistas** that create the illusion of expanse or distant hills. This tends to be comforting and relaxing for the patient.

- **Colorful plantings** are stimulating to the senses. The brighter the flowers and the more of them there are, the better it is for the patient.

- **Fragrance and texture** should also be a part of the Alzheimer's garden. Multiple sensory stimulation is helpful.

- **Caution** must be observed because many plants are poisonous, can cause rashes or possess thorns and spines.

Alzheimer's patients often experience their environment by tasting it.

- **Activity,** if possible, is better than passive stimulation from the garden.

Safe Plants for the Alzheimer's Garden

Beginning on page 25 is a list of edible flowers. Most of these are safe to use in the Alzheimer's garden. The following are also considered safe and provide splashes of color.

Althea (rose of Sharon)
Celosia
Coleus
Dandelion
Daylily
Echinacea
Evening primrose
Hibiscus
Hollyhocks

Impatiens
Platycodon (balloon flower)
Portulaca
Purslane
Rose (thornless)
Sunflower
Torenia
Tuberous begonia

Hibiscus

End of Life and Horticultural Therapy

Hospice programs are perhaps the most misunderstood part of health care. Their role isn't to assist in death, but to help make the end of life as full of comfort and dignity as possible. They make it possible for many of their patients to face the end of life in the familiar setting of home, surrounded by family. Their goal is death with dignity through palliative care and familiar surroundings. For the hospice patient, a plant to care for, to watch grow, to be responsible for, can be a part of that dignity and quality of life.

A stroll through the yard, a park, or botanical garden, even if it's in a wheelchair, is an uplifting experience that stimulates the senses while it gives joy and meaning to life, even at its conclusion. To trim, inhale the fragrance, cut a bouquet, harvest a tomato, share the sun or watch the birds and butterflies is nourishment for the soul, as much as the body.

Creating an after dinner garden can be a pleasant shared experience. Hospice patients and their family members have enjoyed starting pineapples, avocados, mangos, pomegranates, sweet potatoes and dozens of seeds, pits, peelings and exotic fruits, vegetables and nuts.

Many friends and family members find it difficult to visit with someone who is dying, because they don't know what to talk about. The plants, exotic or otherwise, make interesting conversation pieces and open the way for small gifts that can bring great pleasure. The aromatic herbs such as rosemary, mints and lavender can become a useful gardening experience that can be shared with visitors, and caregivers.

The plants release oxygen into the air while they filter out some of the pollutants and noise. They offer learning opportunities, productive diversion, and purpose to an existence that may be reeling out of control.

The following are only a few of the plants that a hospice patient and his or her family caregiver might enjoy growing.

Herbs	Flw. Plants	Foliage Plants
Parsley	African violets	Coffee
Sage	Coleus	Creeping fig
Rosemary	Marigolds	Spider plants
Thyme	Mums	Prayer plant
Mexican tarragon	Petunias	Philodendron
Lemon grass	Salvia	Ferns
Fennel	Torenia	Dracenas
Scented geraniums	Zebra plant	Begonias
Oregano	Gardenia	Pothos
Basil	Amaryllis	Ficus
Mints	Forced bulbs	Pepperomia

There's great value in a *scratch and sniff garden* that gives the opportunity for multiple sensory stimulation. Fawn, a hospice nurse who cared for my mother in her last months was a horticultural therapist without knowing it. She brought cuttings, seedlings and cut flowers. She discussed these with her patient; they shared stories, advice and memories. Fawn was also wise enough to understand the value in gardening as therapy for the caregiver.

Caregivers Need Horticultural Therapy, too

Over twenty-five million Americans are currently devoting a large portion of their lives to caring for a loved one who is confronted with a terminal illness. Millions more are caring for loved ones who face a lifetime with disability. For these dedicated people, the invisible link in health care, a few minutes to escape to the backyard is a treasure. This can be a sanity-saving respite.

For the health care professional, the nurses, aides, hospice volunteers and others, the weight of the job can become too heavy a burden. There are caregiver horticulture programs available that are beneficial to both family caregivers and professional staff. Information is available from the American Horticultural Therapy Association.

Chapter 15
Special Gardens

The child within me,
with unfettered joy climbed the tree,
when no one was looking,
when not a soul was there to see.
I carved an elderberry flute, and down along the garden walk,
accompanied the songbirds as they sang 'round the lily's stalk.
This is my special secret garden, my refuge,
that calm and peaceful place
where I yet can balance sunbeams on my nose
and splash dewdrops on my face.

Scratch & Sniff Gardens

A garden designed to be felt, inhaled, and experienced contains opportunities to employ all the senses at our disposal. A sensory garden is of tremendous value to those with vision impairment, the elderly, children, those suffering from depression, those with brain damage, developmental disabilities, mental and physical limitations, victims of Alzheimer's and other forms of dementia. It's also an opportunity for everyone to experience the therapeutic value of the garden. Simply strolling through such a garden is an active, not passive experience.

To touch, feel textures, let the hands make discoveries; to inhale the varied fragrances and aromas evokes long lost memories as it kindles new interests. Beauty and comfort can be found in the discovery of something new and the comforting recovery of lost images.

Notes on Sensory Gardens

- Match the landscape features, pathways, signs and railings to the intended audience. Wheelchair access, Braille signs, benches for resting, etc.
- Aromatic plants shouldn't be grouped together where their scents mix and overpower the guest to the garden. Blend aromatic plants with plants that have interesting foliage or bark.
- Vegetables and fruit deserve a place in the scratch & sniff garden.
- Raised beds, containers, trellises and arbors can be used to vary the garden's height and give added dimension.
- The sound of running water, music, wind chimes and songbirds can enhance the visit to the garden for the senses.

Author & grandson, Alex, enjoying marigolds

The Touch Pool

Those with dementia, Alzheimer's disease, developmental disabilities, vision impairment, children and all of us who live stress filled lives can enjoy a touch pool. The sense of touch can be comforting, relaxing and more. Simply dipping fingers in the water can also be a therapeutically stimulating way of experiencing the environment. During the observation of a touch pool in a day care facility for Alzheimer's patients, the horticultural therapist found that not only did the patients enjoy the pool, so did the nurses.

A touch pool can be created from any shallow pan, clay saucer or birdbath. It should be a minimum of twenty-four inches in diameter, with a depth of no more than two or three inches.

Into this pool of water we can place a number of things that provide tactile stimulation. It's important to provide a variety of weights, textures and colors. Use your imagination, but avoid small items that can be placed in the mouth or sharp objects that can cause injury. The following are a few suggestions, but this is by no means a complete list.

Washed sand	Sea shells	Water-logged wood
Sandstone	Granite	Quartz or quartzite
Floating flower	Leaves	Large play coins
Piece of chain	Rubber duck	Other toys

If possible, this pool can be an extension of a tabletop fountain. The sound of running water is both calming and stimulating to the senses. Aromatic and colorful plants can be placed around the pool to provide further stimulation, but care must be taken not to use dangerous or poisonous plants.

The pool can be used indoors or out, but because water will be splashed on the floor, care must be taken to prevent falls.

Plants that are Toxic or Dangerous

Young children, individuals with mental limitations and Alzheimer's victims are often tempted to taste and consume the plant material in their presence. To avoid accidental discomfort or poisoning it's best to avoid, or keep from easy reach those specimens that are toxic. If there are any doubts about the safety of a given plant contact your local agricultural extension office or poison control center. The following is a short list of plants that can be a poisoning threat.

amaryllis	elephant ears	periwinkle, vinca
angels trumpet	foxglove	pencil tree, euphorbia
arrowhead	holly berries	philodendron
autumn crocus	hyacinth bulbs	poison ivy
azalea	hydrangea	poke weed
bittersweet	iris	primrose, florist
buckeye	jasmine	privet
buttercup	jimson weed	ranunculus
caladium	lantana camera	rhododendron
calla lily	larkspur	rosary pea
caster bean	mountain laurel	sweet pea
China berry	lily-of-the-valley	tobacco
daffodil	marijuana	tulip
datura	mistletoe	water hemlock
delphinium	nightshade	wisteria
diffenbachia	oleander	yew

Certain common plants found in the vegetable garden can cause problems as well. Tomato and potato leaves contain solanine. Rhubarb leaves contain oxalic acid. Onions, garlic & chives can cause eye irritation, as can chile peppers. Even carrot leaves can cause stomach upset. Cotton and tobacco are both toxic. There are some herbs that can cause problems if ingested including pennyroyal, gotu kola, comfrey, soapwort, and artemisia.

The Night Garden

The garden is different at night. It's as though in every garden there is a duality. The butterflies are asleep while the moths visit the flowers of the night. The cricket's song and the tree frog chorus replace the songbirds' medley. Even the tone of the wind chimes is different, deeper, more resonant. The flowers of day are often spent with sunset, or folded until morning. Certain leaves are also folded as though in prayerful anticipation of dawn's light. The flowers of the night are often sweetly fragrant. Most are light in color, so as to almost glow in the moonlight.

Many of us are reluctant to venture into our gardens in the night, fearful of the unknown and unseen, fearful of the darkness. But there is a serene beauty in the night garden unlike anything we can know in the light of day. The coolness of the air is calming, the sounds don't rush toward us all at once, but glide into our senses one by one. The comforting, reassuring scent of moist air mingles with the flowers and stirs within us all a primeval acceptance of the universe. In the night garden, we are secure in the shadows of the universe, we can see beyond the clouds all the way to the stars, an infinity distant. Time stands motionless in the darkness, granting us the opportunity to relax and catch up with ourselves.

There is a romance in the night garden far more sensual than the same place provides in the afternoon sun. In solitude we can discover ourselves. The blackness illuminates our soul by providing a place and a time for reflection, meditation, an opportunity to know self. A pool captures the moonbeams, and in its ripple makes a million more moons. To sit in the tranquillity of our garden of the night is to know harmony and peace, to be one with beauty.

There are discoveries to be made in the night garden, if we are courageous enough to turn off the lights. The squirrels have retired from their afternoon romps, but field mice, opossum, raccoon, armadillo, even deer find in the darkness their security. Owls, nighthawks and bats rule their airy domain, while the whip-poor-will calls to us.

To best experience and enjoy our night garden, we need to plan ahead and provide clear walkways, and comfortable places to sit. Throughout the garden we can plant the night bloomers like the following:

Night-blooming jasmine

Moon flower vine

Night blooming cereus

Nicotiana (Flowering tobacco)

Datura (Angel's trumpet)

Four o'clocks

Some orchids

Evening scented stocks

Evening primrose

Petunias

Catchfly (Silene)

Honeysuckle

Orchid cactus

One of the great events for the nighttime gardener is the opening of the night blooming cereus, a vining cactus with a blossom that may be a foot in diameter, glowing white and subtly sweet scented. The flower will be pollinated and withered by the next day. But the glory is in the twin gifts, momentary beauty and forever memories. It's even better when friends are invited to share the spectacle of the bud gradually becoming flower.

The night garden is therapy for the individual. It whispers secrets and becomes a place of discoveries. It gently urges us to pause, relax, and reflect on our place in the universe.

Moth visiting night blooming cactus

Chapter 16
Horticultural Therapy in Tomorrow's World

As we enter a new century, and a new millennium, we are faced with serious global problems. The suicidal drive to use up our natural resources, destroy species and eco-systems, to foul the air, water and earth upon which we depend for our very existence, has got to stop. As the global population ages, there will be a decrease in some of the demands humanity places on the environment, but this will be replaced with the need for other resources. The only solution that makes sense in the long range is cooperation on a global scale. This involves all of us combining our efforts to preserve our natural world while we combat hunger and disease. The quality of life isn't increased by possessing our world, but rather, by experiencing it.

One of the avenues toward understanding our place in the web of life can be found in our instinctive need for the people-plant connection. Charles Lewis, in his delightful book, *Green Nature, Human Nature*, explores this unity of life and what it can mean to future generations. Programs like the Eden Alternative will be increasingly popular with the elderly population.

The role of horticultural therapy in the nursing home, assisted living facility, hospitals, and other health care institutions will grow rapidly in the next few years. The logic of this is two fold. First is the desire to give our elderly citizens as much dignity, meaning and quality as we can in the end game of life. The gardening experience helps to do that. Second is the simple fact that senior citizens who engage in gardening activities tend to be healthier, require less medication, and live happier. Horticultural therapy programs are cheaper for nursing homes than medication and doctor's visits.

In mental institutions and substance abuse centers, the HT programs are often one of the most effective parts of the treatment program, and one of the least expensive.

More and more universities and community colleges are offering horticultural therapy training programs. The community as a whole is awakening to the value of parks.

Urban greening and community gardening are bringing people together, and the horticultural therapist is a key element in the success of such programs.

Even the business community is seizing the moment as they make the workplace green. Offices and manufacturing facilities are beginning to employ horticultural therapists as consultants. These businesses know that there is increased productivity, a greater sense of cooperation, decreased absenteeism and fewer labor-management disputes when there is a green place to take a break, walk off the tension or enjoy lunch with co-workers. Enlightened companies are even taking this beyond the passive enjoyment of a park-like setting. They encourage gardening breaks, make space available for staff to grow a cutting garden, cultivate herbs that can garnish their meals, even grow a salad.

Schools are energetically including gardening programs in their curriculums and activities. When they encourage the students to take part in the landscaping of the school grounds, vandalism decreases. Children earn acceptance and praise from the community when they raise food for the local food bank, beautify their school grounds, take flowers to a local nursing home, clean up a park or create a butterfly garden. The most effective of these programs use horticultural therapists either as program leaders or as consultants.

In the future civic organizations, churches, and other institutions will work with horticultural therapists to make a better community, combat hopelessness, strengthen the body, open the mind and liberate the soul.

If you would like to have more information about what a horticultural therapist does, or if you would like to become one, contact the American Horticultural Therapy Association, 909 York St., Denver, CO 70206-3799, or access their web site www.ahta.org.

We can all help our parents, family and friends to lead a richer, fuller and happier life by encouraging health care facilities, social programs and educational institutions to include gardening as therapy. By doing so, we help ourselves and the rest of the world.

Resources

This book was written to provide a somewhat different view of the value of gardening, but this is by no means the only text on the market that explores the role of horticultural therapy. The following are a few more that you might want to read.

Green Nature/Human Nature: The Meaning of Plants in our Lives by Charles Lewis and released in 1996, is one of the most powerful and insightful books on the connection between people and plants ever written. This is a must read for anyone interested in horticultural therapy.

Horticulture as Therapy: Principles and Practice, edited by Pastor, Simson & Strauss and published by Haworth Press in 1997. This is the textbook for the field of horticultural therapy. It is 478 pages overflowing with information. The most comprehensive text on the discipline available.

The Enabling Garden: A guide to Lifelong Gardening, by Gene Rothert was published in 1994 by Taylor Publishing Co. Rothert is one of the foremost authorities in the field and former president of the American Horticultural Therapy Association. This book describes a multitude of ways to make gardening accessible to those of us with handicaps.

The Role of Horticulture in Human Well-Being and Social Development, edited by Diane Relf and published by Timber Press in 1992 this is an in depth study that involves a multi-disciplinary approach to the connection between people and plants. This is a valuable book for everyone who works with plants.

Horticultural Therapy for the Mentally Handicapped, by Daubert & Rothert. Published in 1981, this book contains valuable information from two outstanding experts in the field.

Accessible Gardening: Tips & Techniques for Seniors & the Disabled, by Joan Woy. Published in 1997. This book provides a comprehensive and compassionate personal approach to the garden. She also defines the role of horticulture as therapy.

Accessible Gardening for People with Physical Disabilities: A Guide to Methods, Tools & Plants, by Janeen R. Adil. Published in 1995 by Woodbine House, this is one of the premier how-to books on creating and using accessible gardens. This was written to help bring the joys of gardening to everyone.

The Able Gardener, by Kathleen Yeomans. Published by Story Communications in 1995. This is a great how to book for the beginner.

Able to Garden: A Practical Guide for Disabled and Elderly Gardeners, edited by Peter Please and published in London in 1990, this book provides a wealth of information on effective use of space and resources. It's a collection of works by members of the British Society for Horticultural Therapy.

Creating Eden: The Garden as a Healing Space, by Marilyn Barrett, Ph.D. Was published by Harper Collins in 1992. The author is a psychotherapist who uses the garden as metaphor for life and gardening as a means of self-exploration and discovery.

Garden for Life: Horticulture for People with Special Needs, by Lynn Davis was published by University of Saskatchewan Press in 1994. This is a small book with a mountain of readable information between the covers.

Gardens in Healthcare Facilities: Uses, Therapeutic Benefits and Design, and **Healing Gardens: Therapeutic Benefits and Design Recommendations,** edited by Claire Cooper Marcus, both provide detailed technical information on both the how and why of therapeutic gardening.

Healing Dimensions of People-Plant Relations, edited by Francis, Lindsey & Rice and published by the Office of Environmental Horticulture in 1994. This is a premier resource that explores in depth both the value of HT and the techniques employed.

Gardening Is for Everyone, by Cloet & Underhill was published in London in 1990. This is a great instruction manual for those establishing horticultural therapy programs. The activities and teaching techniques described are an invaluable resource.

A Patch of Eden: America's Inner-City Gardeners, by H. Patricia Hynes and published by Chelsea Green in 1996. This text explores the societal aspects of gardening. It's a great study into the why of community gardening.

A Place to Grow: Voices and Images of Urban Gardeners, edited by David Hassler and published by Pilgrims Press in 1999.

Associations, Agencies and Organizations involved with Horticultural Therapy

American Horticultural Therapy Association (AHTA) at 909 York St., Denver CO 70206-3799, and their web site www.ahta.org has a multitude of books, periodicals and fact sheets available.

American Association of Botanical Gardens and Arboreta at 351 Longwood Rd., Kennet Square, PA 19348, phone (610) 925-2500, web site www.mobot.org/AABGA is also a wealth of information.

The National Gardening Association (NGA), is a valuable resource for teachers interested in school and community projects.

American Community Garden Association (ACGA), 100 N 20th St, 5th Floor, Philadelphia, PA 19103-1495, phone (215) 988-8785 is a great source of information on both how to create community gardens and why it should be done.

City Farmer, Canada's Office of Urban Agriculture, #801-318 Homer St., Vancouver, B.C. V6B 2VB, phone (604) 685-5832, web site www.cityfarmer.org is a valuable resource on community gardening.

This is by no means a complete list. More information can be found at your local library, botanical garden and university.

Horticultural therapy won't solve all the problems of society, but it can open the door to cooperation, acceptance and pride.

It cannot cure all the mental and physical ills that limit our ability to experience and enjoy life to the fullest, but it can provide incentive to try and a means to improve confidence.

It can't reverse the effects of aging, Alzheimer's disease, AIDS, congestive heart failure and other terminal conditions, but it can provide moments of joy and make even the end of life a journey of discovery.

For all of us, the gardening experience can be an exercise in stress relief and a way to find ourselves in the confusing maze of daily life. The garden is an open door to our place in the natural world, a way to connect with our instincts, and a quiet spot where the wounded soul can heal.